QUEEN NITOCRIS

On the front cover is a portrait thought to be of Frances Howard, Countess of Somerset (read about her within), attributed to William Larkin, c. 1615-1620, in the National Portrait Gallery, London. On the back cover is Saskia as Bellona (whose followers were a cruel, bloody bunch) by Rembrandt, 1633; the Metropolitan Museum of Art, the Michael Friedsam Collection, 1931.

There are no portraits of Queen Nitocris; these dresses from the Old Kingdom are borrowed from Queen Mersyankh III.

QUEEN NITOCRIS
wicked around 2175 B.C.

We don't really know much about Queen Nitocris, and historians are still arguing as to whose queen she was, and when. The Greek historian Herodotus tells us what we know about her. (Herodotus is usually called "the father of history," but is also known as "the father of lies," in tribute to the complete falsity of some of his history.)

Herodotus says of Nitocris, "The story was that she ensnared to their deaths hundreds of Egyptians in revenge for the king, her brother, whom his subjects had murdered and forced her to succeed; this she did by constructing an immense underground chamber, in which, under the pretense of opening it by an inaugural ceremony, she invited to a banquet all the Egyptians whom she knew to be chiefly responsible for her brother's death; then, when the banquet was in full swing, she let the river in on them through a large concealed conduit-pipe." As you would expect, this broke up the party.

Herodotus was told that Nitocris did not long survive her revenge. He says that she "flung herself into a room full of ashes, to escape her punishment."

SEMIRAMIS
active about 800 B.C.

Most of what we know about Semiramis comes from a Greek historian, Diodorus of Sicily, who lived about 800 years later than she did. Most of it is also untrue: by the time of Diodorus, two different Assyrian queens had been confused into one woman, and a number of legends had been attached to the figure—some of them stories which have been told about many women who ruled. For example, Semiramis is supposed to have taken the handsomest soldiers in her army as lovers and to have killed each when she wanted a new one.

Diodorus tells us that Semiramis was the daughter of the goddess of love, Ishtar, who fell in love with a handsome young Assyrian and became pregnant. Disgusted with herself for having stooped so low, Ishtar killed her lover, left their child to die in the desert near Ascalon in Palestine, and changed herself into a being with the head of a woman and the body of a fish, removing the possibility of future temptation. You might think that Semiramis' divine birth would make her conspicuous but as all the Assyrian royalty were said to be descended from gods, no one thought much about it.

After being abandoned, she was nursed for a year by doves, then found by a local cowherd who raised her as his daughter. When she was grown, a royal officer named Onnes came to inspect the herds. After inspecting the beautiful Semiramis too, he married her and had two sons by her. "And since he would do nothing without her advice, he prospered in everything."

Onnes was called to serve in the army of King Ninus, who had raised two million men to fight the Bactrians. The army stalled in front of the city of Bactra, which it besieged but could not capture. Onnes, bored with siege life, sent for his wife. When Semiramis arrived, she found a way to capture the impregnable city, and led the troops to the attack herself.

The king, much impressed by this feat, was more impressed by her beauty. He offered to trade Onnes one of his daughters for Semiramis; when Onnes refused, Ninus threatened to blind him. Onnes committed suicide; Ninus married Semiramis; and they had a son, Ninyas. Ninus then died, leaving Semiramis to rule as queen.

She founded the great city of Babylon. Diodorus gives her credit for all the famous buildings of Babylon—the city walls, bridges, reservoirs, palaces, aqueducts and temples, but the Hanging Gardens came later. Among the temples were the great ziggurat, three hundred feet high, which we call the Tower of Babel, and an obelisk one hundred thirty feet tall.

SEMIRAMIS

—the most renowned of all women of whom we have any record.
Diodorus of Sicily

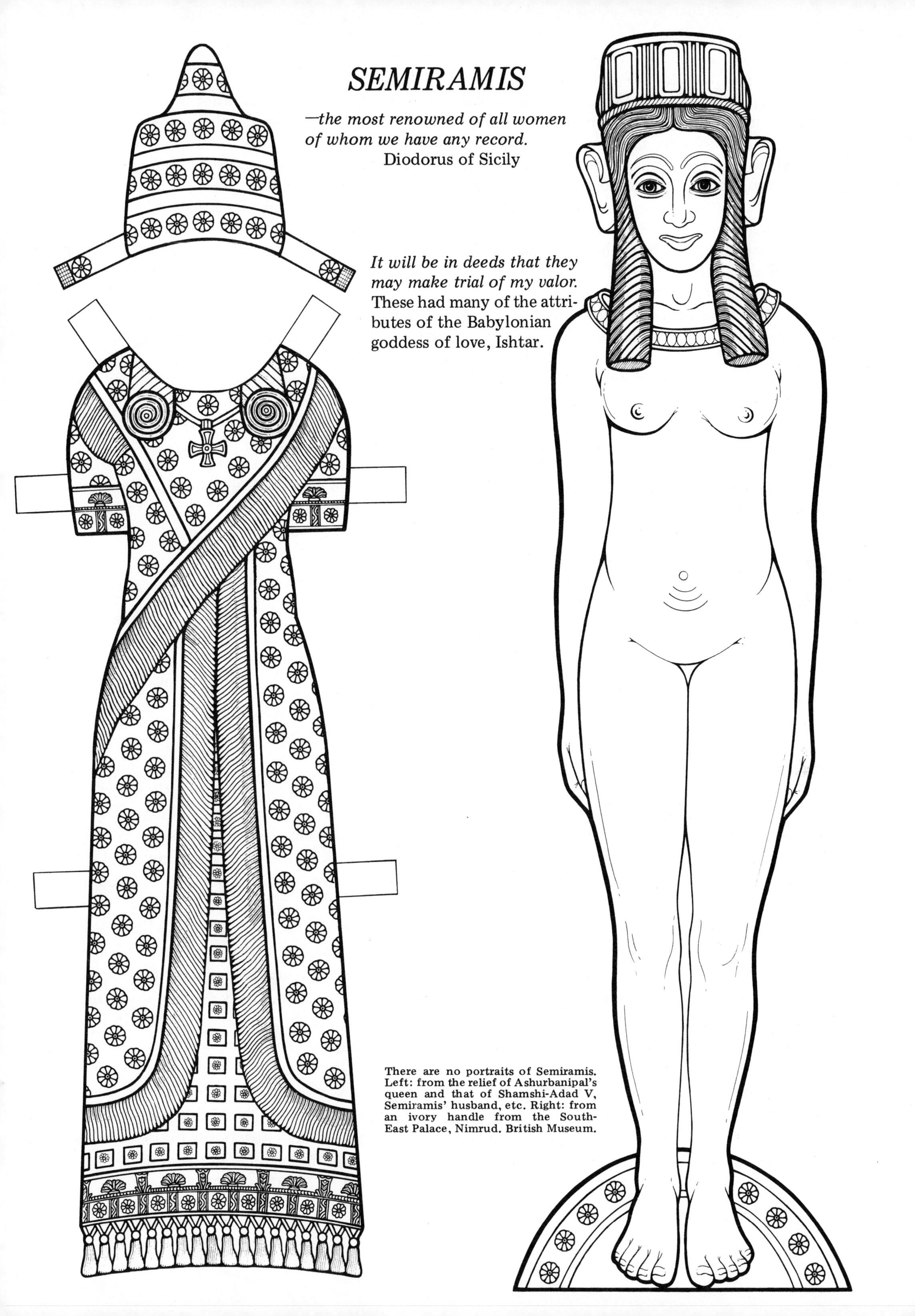

It will be in deeds that they may make trial of my valor. These had many of the attributes of the Babylonian goddess of love, Ishtar.

There are no portraits of Semiramis. Left: from the relief of Ashurbanipal's queen and that of Shamshi-Adad V, Semiramis' husband, etc. Right: from an ivory handle from the South-East Palace, Nimrud. British Museum.

Semiramis also travelled and fought. She visited Egypt and Ethiopia, then decided to win fame by conquering India. But the Indian king had a superweapon which terrified all other troops—elephants. He had a corner on the supply, so no one could counter his forces. Semiramis decided to beat real elephants with dummy elephants, moved by camels inside. These were made in secrecy by workers who were kept prisoner, so that the weapon would be a complete surprise. Semiramis thought that the Indians would be so upset at discovering that their opponents had elephants too that they would all flee.

After three years' preparation, Semiramis took her army of three and a half million men against the Indian king's army of the same size. When the armies met in battle, the Indian horses fled—not from the dummy elephants, but from the unfamiliar smell of the camels within them. But the Indian king rallied his men and their charge routed Semiramis' army. She herself was slightly wounded, and two-thirds of her men were lost. Neither side won anything.

After this war, her son Ninyas wanted to rule. Semiramis, obeying omens from the gods, did not resist: she turned over the government to him and disappeared, having lived sixty-two years and reigned forty-two.

Modern historians take most of the juice out of this story. To begin with, they say, Diodorus's Semiramis is a mixture of two different Assyrian queens, who reigned five generations apart. The first, Sammuramat, whose name means "palace-lady," ruled three years after the death of her husband Shanshi-Adad V, who had reigned from 823 B.C. to 811 B.C. He corresponds to Semiramis' Ninus, the founder of Ninevah (the center of the goddess Ishtar, worshipped like the planet Venus), but some of Ninus's feats were accomplished by Sennacherib, whose wife Naqi'a, the Pure One, who reigned 683-670 B.C., is the second part of Diodorus' Semiramis. After her husband's death Naqi'a held the throne and kept the country together until her grandson Assur-ban-apli was old enough to rule.

Sammuramat seems to have been the queen whose warlike and building exploits are reflected in the story of Semiramis; Naqi'a was more peaceful, but rebuilt Babylon, which her husband had destroyed, much to the annoyance of the god Marduk.

THE EMPRESS MESSALINA
25-48 A.D.

While the Emperor Claudius (10 B.C. -54 A.D.) has the distinction of being the only man to have married *two* of our Infamous Women, he can hardly be said to have enjoyed the experience. Neither of his first two wives suited him: he divorced the second because he suspected her of having committed a murder. But when he traded her in on a third, Messalina, he didn't realize he had traded up to a major-league criminal.

There were lots of things that Claudius didn't realize. His family decided early in his life that he was a bit simple. Unlike the other descendents of the Emperor Augustus, he was not given any major public offices in Rome. As a result, unlike the other grandsons of Augustus, he survived the reigns of his unpleasant uncle Tiberius and his crazy nephew Caligula. When the soldiers finally decided that Caligula was intolerable, and assassinated him, a soldier found Uncle Claudius hiding behind a curtain in the palace. Instead of killing him, the soldier proclaimed him emperor. Everyone was willing to accept Claudius, since they thought he would cause no trouble.

He didn't, but his wives did. Valeria Messalina, his third, was the daughter of a cousin of Claudius. Caligula had Claudius marry her when he was 50, she 15, apparently as a joke. (Caligula was very proud of his sense of humor, and after he became Emperor, many people told him how funny his jokes were. Those who were not amused soon were not around.) Messalina was quite beautiful, and Claudius soon was very much in love with her. After he became Emperor, they had two children, Britannicus and Octavia. Messalina became a major power in the government, and those whom she favored got the best jobs.

MESSALINA

O facinus! O scelus!

But holding power did not satisfy all Messalina's desires. Neither did Claudius. While Roman women in imperial circles were not always faithful to their husbands, Messalina went far beyond the usual quiet love affairs. She had affairs with gladiators, dancers, and other persons most empresses never met. She was a hard woman to refuse: those who turned her down were accused by informers of plotting against the Emperor, and were executed. When Mnestor the actor hesitated, she told Claudius to order him to do as the Empress wished. She took the handsomest men of Rome, and occasionally, for novelty, the ugliest. When looking for new worlds to conquer, she challenged Scylla, a champion prostitute, to a competition: which could wear out more customers? Scylla gave up at dawn, after XXV; Messalina continued tirelessly into the day. The Roman satirist Juvenal describes her as finally going home "tired but never satisfied."

Claudius was the last person in Rome to know what his wife was doing. She went too far when she fell in love with Gaius Silius, the handsomest man in Rome. After making him divorce his wife, she lived openly with him, redecorating his home with furniture from the Imperial Palace. Finally she decided to celebrate a bigamous marriage with him, after which they would get rid of Claudius. The Roman historian Tacitus says, "She craved the name of wife because it was outrageous and thus the greatest satisfaction to a sensation-seeker."

Claudius' freedmen secretaries, who knew that if he were killed, they would be too, informed Claudius of Messalina's wedding. He sent his guards to arrest the guests at the bacchanalian feast she was giving in celebration. The drunks scattered, and Messalina tried to reach Claudius to appeal to his love. No one would help her: she was

Head: Ny Carlsberg Glyptothek, Copenhagen. Body: Lateran, Rome.

"not pitied, so hideous were her crimes, by a single person," says Tacitus. She was sent a message that troops were coming. She was supposed to commit suicide: even her mother urged her to die honorably before the troops killed her. "But in that lust-ridden heart there was no trace of decency; her tears and laments continued when the men broke the doors by force," Tacitus tells us. Even now she lacked courage to kill herself: the officer commanding the troops stabbed her. The news of her death was brought to Claudius at his dinner. He did not ask how she had died, but called for more wine.

THE EMPRESS AGRIPPINA
15-59 A.D.

After discovering Messalina's crimes, Claudius told his soldiers to kill him if he was such a fool as to marry again. But he did, and they didn't. This time he found the one woman in Rome who was worse than Messalina, his niece Agrippina.

She was the daughter of Claudius' brother, the great general Germanicus, and a sister of the Emperor Caligula. She had been married to Gnaeus Domitius Ahenobarbus ("Bronzebeard"). The Roman historian Suetonius calls this husband "a wholly despicable character": Agrippina's son by him, Domitius, better known as the Emperor Nero, was evidently a chip off these two old blocks.

When Caligula became Emperor, he decided he was a god, and he imitated the domestic lives of the gods by sleeping with his 3 sisters, Drusilla, Livilla, and Agrippina. He also set up a brothel in his palace, to raise money, and sold his sisters for high prices. Ultimately he got tired of having them around the court, and sent Livilla and Agrippina in exile to a small island where they were forced to earn their bread by diving for sponges. Claudius, who was kind-hearted, allowed the girls to return to Rome when he took the throne.

After Messalina's death, Agrippina began to make up to Uncle Claudius. Pallas, Claudius's financial secretary, who was her lover, pushed her as a candidate for empress. She was intelligent and could help with the work of governing; since her son was a grandson of Germanicus, he was a worthy member of the imperial family; she might have another son, to give the Emperor an heir not the child of Messalina; and as a rich member of the imperial family, it would be unsafe to let her marry anyone else who might get ambitious for the imperial throne. Claudius accepted these arguments, especially after Agrippina seduced him. There was still one problem: Roman law defined such an arrangement as incest. But the Roman Senate had been well trained in servility by its dealings with Tiberius and Caligula. When a spokesman for the Emperor suggested the incestuous marriage, they urged it unanimously as being for the good of the country.

Agrippina quickly became the main power in the government. The Roman tradition was that women belonged in the home, so many objected. Tacitus says, "Complete obedience was given to a woman. But, unlike Messalina, she did not dabble in politics for fun. She brought to it an almost masculine sense of service; her seriousness was obvious, as was, often, her arrogance. She lived chastely, except in order to gain more power. Her passion to acquire wealth was enormous, for it could lead to the acquisition of further power.

Agrippina persuaded Claudius to marry his daughter Octavia to her son Nero. She prepared to make him, not Claudius' son Britannicus, the heir to the throne. She also guarded her own position by having murdered women whose beauty Claudius had praised. Officials whose loyalty was to Claudius were replaced by her own men.

When she decided it was time to remove Claudius, poison was her chosen method. She gave Claudius a particularly choice mushroom from a dish she was eating: it was the only poisoned one. Claudius was given a fine funeral, and proclaimed a god. Nero, another imperial humorist, in later years used to get laughs by referring to mushrooms as "the food of the gods."

Agrippina now seemed to have total power. Her son, who appreciated what she had done for him, gave as the watchword for his guard, "the best of mothers." But Nero began to resent his mother's control. She wanted an open share in the government, which the Romans would have thought scandalous. She thwarted Nero's love affairs, forbid him to do as he chose, and threatened that she would expose his treatment of her, and make Britannicus emperor in his place.

AGRIPPINA

—ready for a swim.

The best of mothers!
—Nero

From a statue of Agrippina, Archaeological Museum, Venice.

From a statue of Diana, Archaeological Museum, Seville.

Nero ended this threat by poisoning 14-year-old Britannicus at the imperial table. He cunningly bypassed the boy's taster, appointed to protect him from poison, by having him handed a tasted cup in which the liquid was too hot. A servant poured in cold water, which contained poison. Britannicus took one sip, went into convulsions, and died instantly. Nero "lay back unconcernedly," claiming that Britannicus was merely having an epileptic fit. The Empress Octavia, Britannicus's sister, though young, "had learnt to hide sorrow, affection, every feeling. After a short silence the banquet continued."

Now Nero threw Agrippina out of his palace. Hired informers accused her of plotting Nero's death. But Agrippina, who had bravery enough for anything, faced down the charges. Now Nero fell in love with Sabina Poppaea, who wanted to become empress. Agrippina opposed this, and the two women fought for control of Nero. Agrippina went so far as to sleep with her son to retain her influence. But Nero decided he would have to kill her to be free of her. Avoiding poison, which would remind people of the fate of Claudius and Britannicus, he tried several ingenious devices. All failed. Finally he planned a shipwreck. He prepared a ship which would collapse at sea, then gave a banquet of reconciliation for his mother. He treated her with great respect, then ushered her to her ship and bade her farewell, kissing her affectionately on the eyes and bosom. At this point, no doubt, he felt his problems were ended.

When the planned accident occurred, Agrippina's two companions were killed. She was wounded, but swam to shore anyhow—her past as a sponge-diver proved handy. She sent a messenger to inform her son of her escape, pretending to have no suspicions of his guilt so that she would have time to plan her counterstroke. Nero was terrified: he had reason to know that her revenge was likely to be deadly. He framed her messenger by accusing him of attacking the emperor, then sent a freedman to kill his mother. Her last words are supposed to have been, "Strike here," as she pointed to the womb from which Nero had come.

EMPRESS WU
625-705

The Empress Wu, the only female reigning sovereign in the long history of China, murdered three of her own children as well as most of her husband's relatives to get to the throne. She had herself declared a reincarnation of Buddha, and she scandalized the court by her affair with an ex-wrestler whom she had named abbot of a great Buddhist temple. In the end, she was overthrown by her ministers, who were disgusted by her shameless behavior with her two favorites, the handsome Jang brothers; she was eighty at the time.

Wu Meiniang was the daughter of a general in the service of the first T'ang emperor, T'ai-tsung. She joined the emperor's household at fourteen and eventually became one of the 27 tsairen, the lowest-ranking official concubines. When T'ai-tsung died in 649, Wu and the other court ladies were sent to a Buddhist convent, as was the custom. The new empress, Wang, brought Wu back to court to distract Emperor Kao-tsung, who was lavishing too much attention on his favorite, Lady Shiao. Kao-tsung was enchanted with Wu, though his court was horrified: since Wu had been his father's mistress, Kao-tsung was committing incest. Wu's first child by the Emperor was a daughter, born in 651. Wu strangled the infant and put the blame on Empress Wang. Kao-tsung believed the lie, since he couldn't imagine that Wu would kill her own child; he knew better later. The Emperor withdrew his favor from Wang, and Wu bided her time until 655, when she planted a wooden figure with a nail through its chest under poor Wang's bed. That did it; Kao-tsung divorced Wang, imprisoned her (along with Lady Shiao for good measure) on a charge of practising black magic against the emperor, and married Wu.

The new Empress was afraid that Kao-tsung might begin to regret Wang and Shiao—as indeed he did—so she ordered them whipped and their hands and feet cut off. To make sure that they wouldn't bother her again, she had them thrown into the palace wine vats. "Let their bones and marrow melt in drunken ecstasy," she said. She was troubled by their ghosts, and persuaded the Emperor to build her a new palace to get away from them.

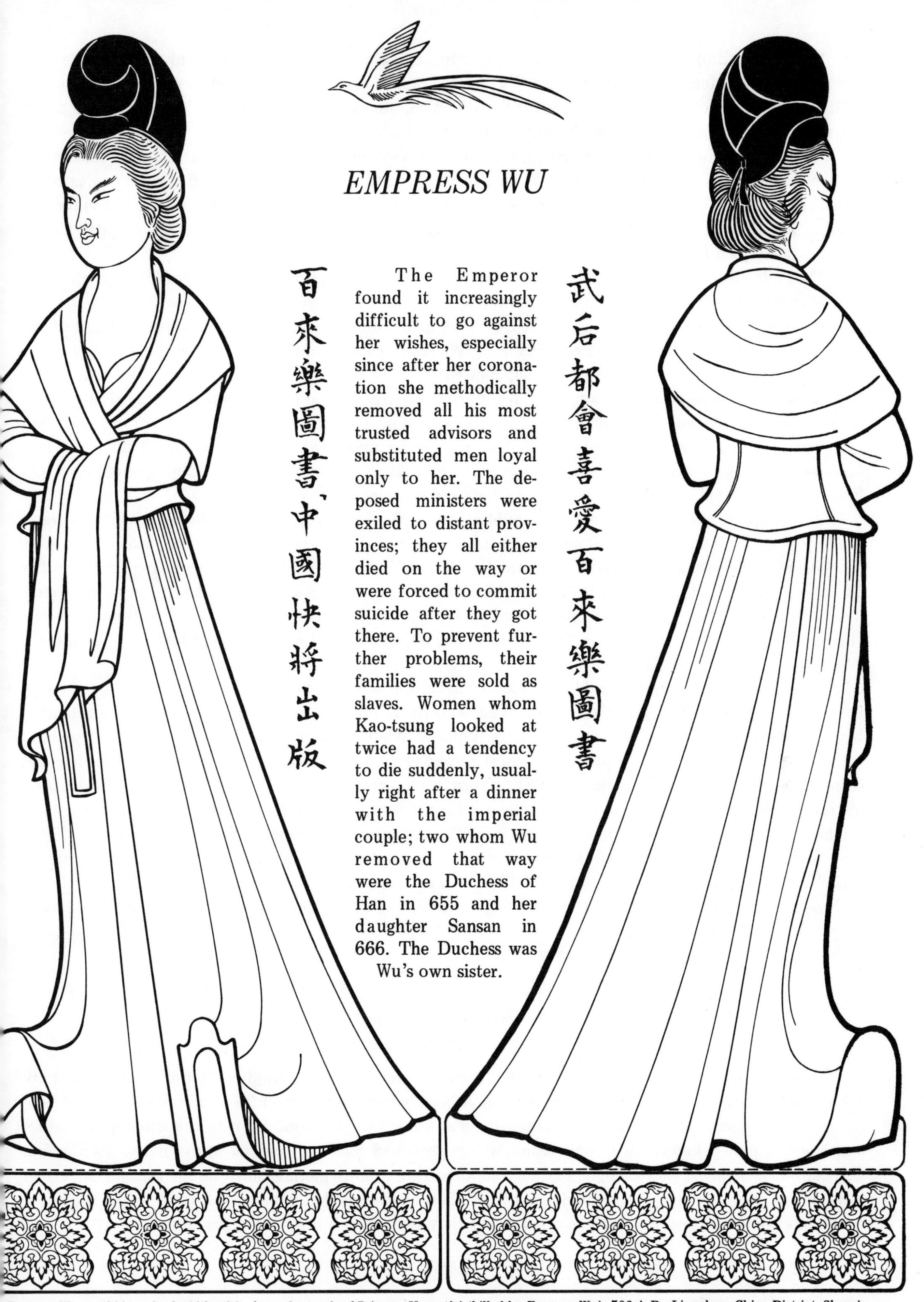

EMPRESS WU

武后都會喜愛百來樂圖書

The Emperor found it increasingly difficult to go against her wishes, especially since after her coronation she methodically removed all his most trusted advisors and substituted men loyal only to her. The deposed ministers were exiled to distant provinces; they all either died on the way or were forced to commit suicide after they got there. To prevent further problems, their families were sold as slaves. Women whom Kao-tsung looked at twice had a tendency to die suddenly, usually right after a dinner with the imperial couple; two whom Wu removed that way were the Duchess of Han in 655 and her daughter Sansan in 666. The Duchess was Wu's own sister.

百來樂圖書、中國快将出版

Empress Wu would have looked like this, from the tomb of Princess Yung-t'ai (killed by Empress Wu), 706 A.D., Ling-shan, Chien District, Shensi.

In 664, the Emperor had the first in a long series of paralytic strokes. He was only 36, but life with Lady Wu was wearing. As he grew weaker, Wu asserted herself more and more in affairs of state. He died in 683, but long before that she was the real ruler of China, already scheming to have the title as well as the power, even if she had to murder a few more of her own children to get it.

Wu had four sons by Kao-tsung. Hung, the eldest, was intelligent and courageous. When he objected to the treatment of his brother Jer's wife—Wu had had her locked in a small house and starved to death—he too died suddenly, after a banquet with his parents in 672. Shien, the second son, was also a brave and honest man. He complained about his mother's affair with a palace astrologer in 680, so she stripped him of his titles and exiled him to far-away Szechuan.

That left Jer, the third son, to become emperor when Kao-tsung finally escaped from Wu for good. Jer proved stubborn, so Wu deposed him after a reign of 54 days and substituted Dan, the youngest son. Jer was banished to Hopei and Dan was allowed to be emperor but kept imprisoned in an isolated part of the vast palace. After completing these arrangements, Wu sent a captain of the guard to Szechuan to "protect" the ex-crown prince. Shien was forced to hang himself.

Ruling in the name of her son Dan, Wu started a purge of the late Emperor's family. Her corrupt judges convicted dozens of T'ang princes of treason, using confessions extorted by torture, and then executed or exiled them (the exiled ones died anyway, either murdered or forced to commit suicide). Their families were also killed, or sold into slavery. By 690, after eliminating any possible competition, the Empress Wu declared herself the sole ruler of China and founder of the Chou dynasty.

The Empress took great care of her public image. She had written two books before her marriage, "Lives of Model Women" and "Domestic Duties of Women." She chose Wu Tsertien, which means Wu Modeled-after-Heaven, as her coronation name. By 688, she had become Shengmu Shenhuang (Holy Mother Divine Sovereign) and in 690 she had herself declared a reincarnation of the Buddha Maitreya, graciously descending from heaven to rule the fortunate Chinese people. When she formally came to the throne, she changed her title again, this time to Shengshen Huangdi (Holy Spirit Emperor) and raised her ancestors for seven generations to imperial rank, thus getting her dynasty off to a good start.

While she was making this public parade of virtue, she was scandalizing the court by her open liason with an enormous former wrestler named Feng, known as Little Precious. Wu renamed him Embracing Righteousness and made him abbot of the huge Buddhist White Horse Temple. Their affair lasted from 684 to 694, and the Abbot became one of the most powerful men in China. He grew tired of her in time and stopped satisfying her private demands. She, in turn, took a new lover and slighted Feng in public. He took his revenge by setting fire to the great temple within the palace walls that Wu had built for him. In return, she had him killed. She also dropped Buddhism for Confucianism and changed all her titles again.

She spent her last years with the Jang brothers, two beautiful young men who became her favorites in 697. Worn out by carousing, she was unable to resist a palace coup in 705 which put Jer back on the throne as Emperor Chung-tsung and restored the T'ang dynasty. She died soon after at eighty, of natural causes, amazingly enough.

EMPRESS IRENE
751-803

Empress Irene of Byzantium is also St. Irene to the Eastern Orthodox Church, and is the only Infamous Saint we have included. She grew up in Athens; when she was seventeen, in 768, she married Leo, the heir of Emperor Constantine V. Constantine was known for his opposition to the worship of statues and icons, a policy known as "iconoclasm" which provoked bitter arguments in the Byzantine Empire. Constantine's enemies, who thought that anyone objecting to holy pictures must be against religion, called Constantine "Copronymus," a name derived from their allegation that he relieved himself in the baptismal font while being baptized. Most of the other things they said about him were less printable.

THE EMPRESS IRENE

—the unnatural mother, who may not easily be paralleled in the history of crimes. Gibbon

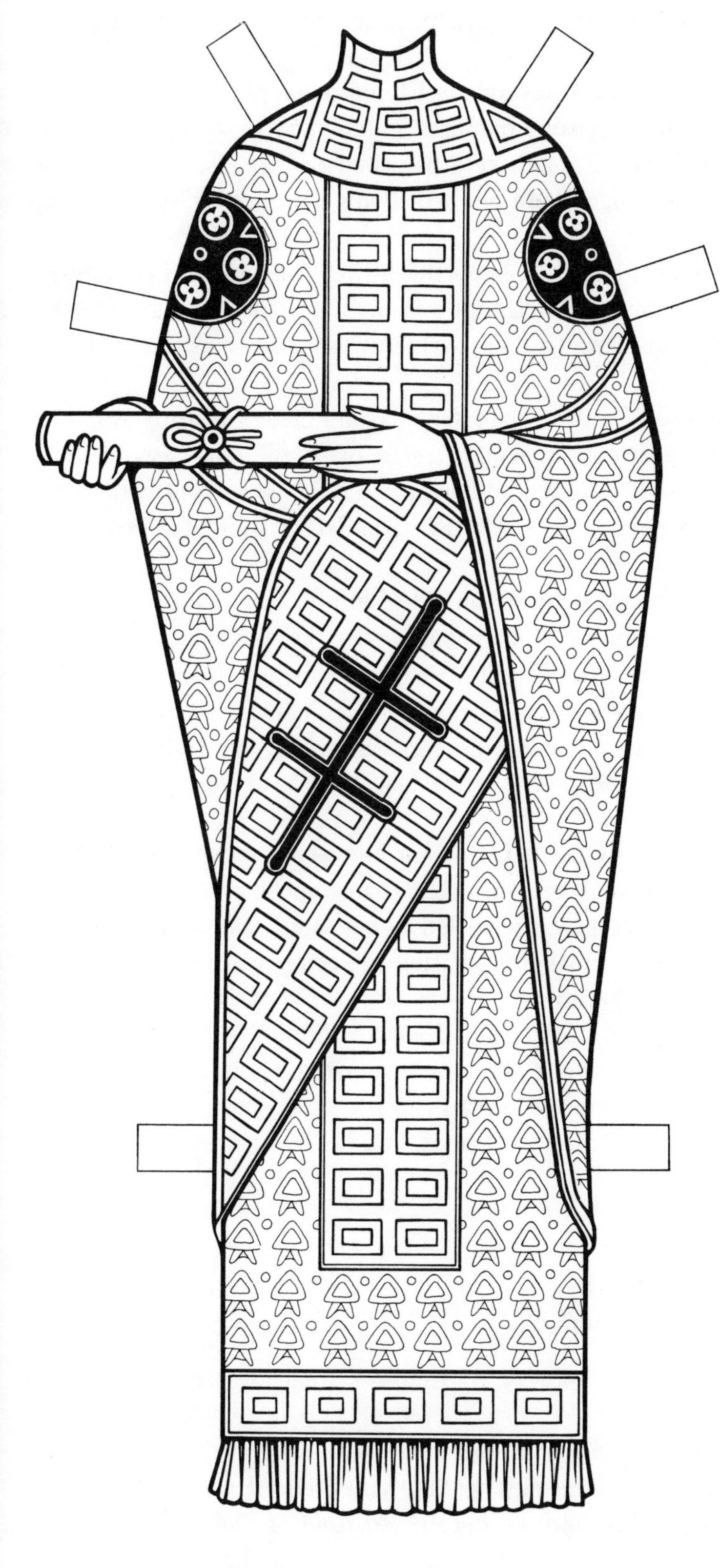

From the *Pala d'Oro*, Saint Mark's, Venice.

From the mosiac in Sancta Sophia; Constantinople, c. 1118.

When Constantine died in 775, the sickly Leo ascended the throne. He lasted only five years. At his death Irene and their ten-year-old son Constantine VI reigned jointly, with Irene controlling things. She reversed her husband's iconoclastic policy. There were some threats to her rule, mostly from her husband's half-brothers, Christophorus, Nicephorus, Nicetus, Anthemus, and Eudocimus. The five stooges, as we shall call them to save space, were harmless, inert, and a bit simple. They lacked the initiative to form plots themselves, but others who plotted used them as figureheads. Just after Irene ascended the throne, a plot to make one stooge emperor was discovered. Because priests were not eligible to rule, Irene forcibly ordained all five stooges, and made them serve the Imperial Court mass on Christmas, to demonstrate that they had left politics.

Another plot on behalf of the stooges surfaced in 792. Constantine VI, annoyed, blinded Nicephorus, and cut out the tongues of the other four. He felt that as visibly damaged goods the five stooges would be less usable as figureheads. After another plot in 797, the stooges were banished to Athens, Irene's home town. In 799, after another plot, the four remaining stooges were blinded. Being a pretender to the throne involved occupational hazards.

When Constantine reached the age to rule, Irene wanted to keep the power for herself. Constantine objected. In 790 Constantine plotted with friends to overthrow the power of Stauricius, the eunuch who was Irene's chief minister. They also wanted to banish Irene to Sicily, which was regarded as the back end of beyond.

Irene and Stauricius discovered the plot, banished Constantine's friends, and made the army swear an oath to Irene: "As long as you live, we will not receive your son to reign over us." They swore, then dethroned Irene in favor of Constantine. Stauricius was whipped and banished, and Irene confined to her own palace. But within two years she managed to regain her son's favor, and that simpleton made her co-empress again.

Constantine lost popularity by divorcing his empress to marry a maid of honor. Irene plotted with his troops, and they sabotaged Constantine's campaign against the Saracens so that he would not regain his popularity by winning a victory. In 797 the troops in Constantinople tried to assassinate Constantine. He escaped, but some of his advisors, who were secretly of Irene's party, betrayed him to her. He was imprisoned in the room in which he had been born, and while he was sleeping, daggers were plunged into his eyes. To everyone's surprise, he survived. In fact, he outlived the next four emperors, into the reign of Michael II, "The Stammerer."

Irene now reigned alone, but the court was divided by fights for power between the two eunuchs who advised her, Stauricius and Aetius. She had no policies of her own, other than opposing iconoclasm, and was entirely controlled by her favorites. Her policy on icons was what led to her sainthood: apparently the church felt that she was right on the main issue, and that a mother is entitled to keep her son in line.

In 802 the noblemen of Byzantium got bored with her incompetence, and chose one of their number, Nicephorus, as Emperor. Irene gave up quietly, asking only for permission to continue to live as a private citizen in her palace. Nicephorus promised her that she could if she would tell him where she had hidden the Imperial treasures. When she gave them to him, he banished her to the Isle of Lesbos, where she was forced to earn her living spinning wool. She died there of disgruntlement, and her successors proceeded to make her reign look like the good old days.

EADBURGHA

at her worst around 802

Queen Eadburgha, who seems to have been a contemporary of Empress Irene, was nasty in a less sophisticated way.

We don't know when Eadburgha was born, but she was the daughter of Offa, King of the Mercians. In 789 she married Beorhtric, or Brihtric, depending on which monk's spelling you prefer. He was King of the West Saxons, who lived in the southwestern corner of England; he became so fond of Eadburgha that she

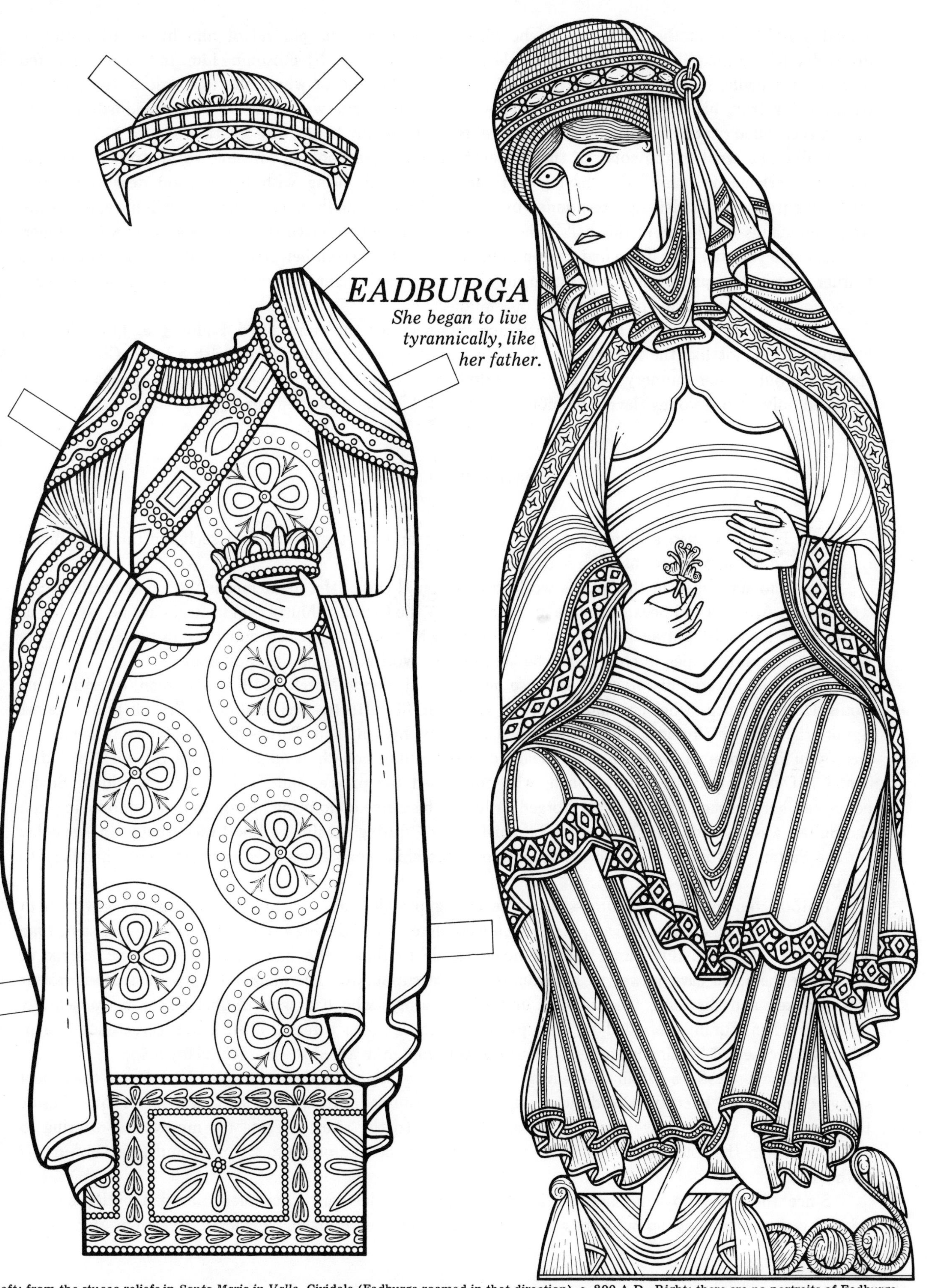

Left: from the stucco reliefs in *Santa Maria in Valle*, Cividale (Eadburga roamed in that direction), c. 800 A.D. Right: there are no portraits of Eadburga, but she would have dressed quite like this, which is from an ivory of later date. Victoria & Albert Museum. The spare crown is from a similar ivory, Louvre.

gained great power in the kingdom. If she disliked someone, she got rid of him by accusing him of disloyalty to the king; if that failed, she would deal more directly, by poisoning him. In 802 she prepared poison for a young man who was a favorite of her husband's, and of whom she was jealous. Her husband took a drink from his friend's cup and soon the widow Eadburgha was asked to leave the kingdom. After having been ruled over by her, the West Saxons refused to give any king's wife the title of Queen.

Eadburgha went to the court of the Emperor Charlemagne, looking for new worlds to conquer. She offered Charlemagne many gifts, having had the foresight to bring with her a good deal of her late husband's treasury. Charlemagne responded by saying, "Choose, Eadburgha, which you will have, me or my son, who stands beside me in this hall." She answered that she preferred the son, because he was younger. Charlemagne told her that if she had chosen him, he would have given her his son; as it was, she would have neither. But one suspects that his question may not have had a right answer: at any rate, Charlemagne got rid of Eadburgha by making her the abbess of a nunnery.

The monks who record her story do not say whether the nuns liked Eadburgha; but evidently Eadburgha did not like the nunnery's style of life, as she was soon discovered with a lover. Charlemagne threw her out of her nunnery, and she is reported to have ended her life begging in the streets of Pavia, attended only by one young slave. The monks felt that this certainly served her right.

SHAJAR AL-DURR
?-1257

Few Islamic women ever had a chance to achieve Infamy: they were kept secluded in the women's quarters, and not allowed to interfere with the affairs of men.

One who succeeded in that man's world was Shajar al-Durr. (Her name means "string of pearls.") She was born in Armenia and became a slave in the harem of the Caliph al-Musta Sim in Baghdad: he gave her as a present to his vassal, Sultan al-Salih Aiyub of Egypt, who found Shajar very much to his taste. Shajar bore the Sultan a son, who died in childhood; she became his favorite wife, and his Sultanah.

But Shajar entered history only because her husband died in March 1249, at a moment of crisis. King Louis IX of France, who was later made a saint for his efforts, was leading a French army against Egypt—the Seventh Crusade. When Aiyub died suddenly, his only son, Turan-shah, was far away, serving as viceroy in Mesopotamia. If Aiyub's army learned of the Sultan's death, it might collapse. So, with the aid of Jamal al-Din Mohren, the chief eunuch, who controlled the palace, and Fakhr al-Din, a soldier, Shajar concealed her husband's death. They forged orders in his name appointing his son as heir, announcing that the Sultan was ill, and naming Fakhr to be chief general during his illness. Food was brought in every day for the Sultan, and Shajar kept up the deception: meanwhile a messenger sped to bring Turan-shah back to Egypt.

It took ten months for Turan-shah to reach Egypt: all that time Shajar held Egypt's government together. By the time Turan arrived, the French were defeated, and King Louis, who was a better saint than general, was captured. But Turan showed no gratitude to those who had saved his kingdom: instead of rewarding them, he gave power to his friends from Mesopotamia. The Mameluk corps of soldiers—slaves from Turkey and Circassia, the proudest unit of the army, who had won the battles—were particularly offended when Turan responded to their protests with drunken threats. Then Turan threatened Shajar, whom he accused of holding his father's treasures from him. She asked the Mameluks for help.

On May 2, 1250, as Turan was leaving a banquet, a group of Mameluks headed by Baibars, their most savage commander, burst in with drawn swords. They wounded Turan, who fled to a wooden tower beside the Nile. They set the tower on fire; Turan jumped into the river, begging for mercy and offering to abdicate. When the soldiers' arrows failed to kill him, Baibars jumped into the river and finished him off with his sabre.

Since there was no adult heir of the royal family, Shajar was proclaimed Sultanah of Egypt. She reigned eighty days, but her subjects were disturbed at the idea of having a woman over them. Her former

There are no portraits of Shajar al-Durr, but this contemporary dress and the crowns are close to what she would have worn. From a 13th-century astronomical manuscript in the Bibliothèque nationale, Paris, Ms. Arabe 2489.

master, the Caliph, offered to send them a man to rule since they had no men among them. The Mameluk amirs decided that their senior officer, Izz ad-Din Aibek would marry Shajar and become Sultan, and Shajar promptly married him. A six-year-old child, al-Ashroof, a relative of the late Sultan, was made co-Sultan, but he soon came to a bad end.

Although Aibek was Sultan, Shajar continued to control the country. She helped Aibek get rid of his Mameluk rivals, who were exiled or killed. But Aibek tired of being second, and quarrelled with his wife. This was foolish of him: Shajar resented his ingratitude, and decided Aibek was dispensable. In April 1257, after a ball game in the royal palace in Cairo, she ordered his eunuchs to murder Aibek while he was bathing. The story was given out that Aibek had died a natural death, but the truth leaked out. Shajar had fewer supporters than she had thought, and her supporters decided to sacrifice her to prevent civil war. After Aibek's death, Shajar was beaten to death with wooden shoes by the slave women of Aibek's first wife. Her body was thrown from a tower.

QUEEN ISABELLA OF ENGLAND
1292-1358

In 1308, when Isabella was 12, her father, King Philip IV of France, married her to King Edward II of England, who was 25. This was her bad luck.

Edward II had been raised strictly by his terrifying father, perhaps the greatest warrior in the Plantagenet line. When Edward I died at 69, his son was 23, and ready to enjoy himself. Although he was tall, golden-haired, and very handsome, he was not prepared to pay much attention to his young wife. As a teenager he had fallen in love with Piers Gaveston, a handsome older knight from Gascony, a part of France owned by the English kings. He wanted to give everything he had to Gaveston. Edward I prevented this by banishing Gaveston, but when Edward II became king, he brought back Gaveston, made him Earl of Cornwall, and gave him his niece in marriage. Gaveston became Edward's principal advisor and closest friend—a profitable position. The English barons were furious: they wanted their share of the king's gifts; they thought only nobly born Englishmen—themselves—should advise the king; they disliked Frenchmen; and they hated Piers. He rubbed in his power. He dressed beautifully, and looked more handsome and elegant then they did. But worst of all, he was a skillful knight: they wanted to beat him up and humiliate him at tournaments, but instead he beat them, then laughed at them.

Isabella did not enjoy her position. She wrote to her father, "I am the most wretched of wives," and told him that the King was "an entire stranger to my bed." When the poet Marlowe wrote a play about her husband 300 years later, he has her moan ". . . the king regards me not, but doats upon the love of Gaveston."

The barons united against Gaveston, and demanded the king banish him. He did so, twice, but each time called Piers back as soon as the lords stopped pressuring him. In 1312 the lords rebelled against the king, captured Gaveston, and beheaded him. In the reaction against this murder, the king regained his power. That same year Isabella gave birth to an heir to the throne, later to be Edward III.

After Gaveston's loss, the king found a new favorite, Hugh Despenser, a baron from the Welsh marches. Hugh was greedy and grasping; people said he led the king "like a cat after a straw." Hugh and his father ran the government capably to benefit themselves and the king. They even fired Isabella's French servants to save money for themselves. By 1321 the barons were urging Edward to banish the Despensers. He did, briefly, but then recalled them when the pressure was off.

By this time Isabella seems to have begun a love affair with a major enemy of her husband's, a Welsh baron, Roger Mortimer of Wigmore. She met him because Mortimer was a prisoner in the Tower of London, which at this time was the principal residence of the royal family. In 1323 Mortimer made a spectacular escape from the Tower. He dug a hole through the wall of his room, passed the guards (who had been drugged), went over the wall with a rope ladder, crossed the moat, and went off to France on a boat which waited for him on the Thames. Since most prisons do not offer the prisoners holes in their walls, drugged guards, and rope ladders, many people suspected that the Queen had helped him.

QUEEN ISABELLA OF ENGLAND
"The She-Wolf of France"

From the Psalter of Queen Isabella, Bayerische Staatsbibliothek, Munich.

Isabella soon found an excuse to join Mortimer in France. Her brother, the King of France, called upon Edward to come to France and do homage for the French possessions of the English crown. Edward did not want to leave England: if he left his favorites, the Despensers, to run the country, he was afraid of what the barons would do to them; if he took the Despensers, he was afraid of what the barons would do to the country. So he accepted Isabella's suggestion that she could go as his ambassador: he had no use for her in England anyhow. Isabella went, and told Edward to send over their son, who could do homage in his place. When the Prince arrived, Isabella threw off the mask: she was going to lead a rebellion against her husband, with the aid of her lover Mortimer.

In 1326 Isabella and her foreign troops landed in England. Everyone supported them; the Despensers were captured and killed; Edward was made a prisoner, and forced in 1327 to abdicate in favor of his son. Since the Prince was not of age, Isabella and Mortimer ran the country for him as they chose. The arrogant Mortimer used his power to the full. He feared that the dethroned king would become the figurehead of a rebellion against his power, so decided Edward must go. His jailers kept the ex-king in cells filled with "mire and puddle," hoping he would die. Edward's strong Plantagenet body withstood all mistreatment, but in 1327 he was murdered in Berkeley Castle.

After Edward's death, Mortimer's power was unquestioned. Even Edward III, the nominal king, could not prevent Mortimer from executing one of his uncles. But in 1330 young Edward planned to take over himself. His friends entered Nottingham Castle, where the Royal household was staying, through a secret tunnel. They captured Mortimer as the Queen cried, "Have pity on the gentle Mortimer." Others had never found him gentle, and they executed him. Edward did not kill his mother, but she was sent away from the court. The last 28 years of her life were spent in quiet seclusion in the English countryside.

JOANNA OF NAPLES
1327-1382

Naples has had many cruel rulers, but the Neapolitans boast particularly of wicked Queen Joanna: she had, they say, many lovers, killed when she tired of them, and many husbands treated similarly.

Her grandfather, King Robert I, left her Naples and Provence when he died in 1343. Many of Joanna's relatives felt that the responsibility of ruling was too great for such a young girl, and were eager to take it from her. One such relative was her husband and second cousin, Andrew of Hungary, to whom Joanna had been married when she was seven. The two had been raised separately, and as teenagers disliked each other. Andrew had renounced any claim to be called king, or to hold power, in his marriage contract; but now that he had grown up, he wanted control. Joanna objected.

One night Andrew was called out of the royal bedroom to receive a messenger. Outside the room he was attacked: several men dragged him out onto the terrace, put a silk cord (said to have been made by Joanna) about his neck, and suspended him from the balcony, while other conspirators hung from his feet to strangle him more quickly.

Andrew had been so obnoxious that many people had reason to kill him. No one ever proved that Joanna was implicated, but most people believed the worst.

With Andrew dead, Joanna's other relatives had a chance to get into the act. In Naples she had more second cousins, belonging to two powerful families, the lords of Durazzo and Taranto, each of which felt it should have the Neapolitan throne. Charles of Durazzo, who was married to Joanna's sister and heir Marie, spread the story that Joanna had killed Andrew, hoping that Joanna would be deposed in favor of his wife. The Taranto family supported Joanna to oppose the Durazzos, but the two brothers, Robert and Louis, fought each other for the right to marry Joanna and take over her power. Robert ran ahead at first, and made Joanna his mistress, but lacked staying power; Louis replaced him and married Joanna in 1347. Meanwhile Andrew's father, King Louis I ("the Great") of Hungary decided to bring his army to Naples to avenge his son's murder and console himself by taking the throne himself.

Joanna and Louis of Tarento had to flee to Provence. After she sold Avignon to the Pope, he approved

JOANNA OF NAPLES

of her new marriage, absolved her of guilt for Andrew's death, and helped her regain Naples. But Louis of Tarento turned out to be a poor bargain too: he also wanted to rule, and kept his wife almost a prisoner.

Meanwhile there was a struggle for possession of Marie, the heir. While Louis of Hungary held Naples,

Joanna sometimes wore armor: after A. del Castagno, S. Apollonia, Florence.

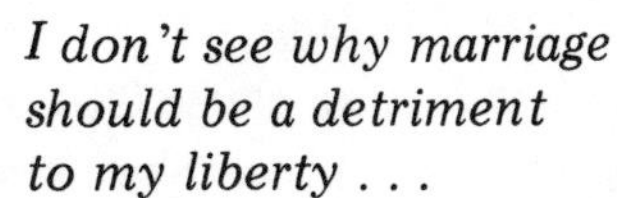

From *Status de l'Ordre de St. Esprit*, 1352. Bibliothèque nationale.

he executed Marie's husband: she and her children fled half-naked into the night. A few years later, when Louis was back in Hungary, his wife died: he proposed to marry Marie, but before this could happen a powerful baron, Huges des Baux, captured Marie, and had his son Robert marry her by force. Louis and Joanna agreed on few things, but they agreed in disliking this marriage. They imprisoned Robert. When Louis and Joanna were out of the castle one day Marie went down to her husband's dungeon and had him killed while she watched.

Historians describe Louis as violent, miserly, cruel, timid, ungrateful, incompetent, and treacherous. The best thing he did from Joanna's point of view was to die in 1362; Joanna, who like Henry VIII, never knew when to leave well enough alone, married again. This time she picked James, King of Majorca, who had just escaped from a Spanish prison. After a few weeks of married life, Joanna decided he should have stayed there: much of the time he was insane—particularly when drunk—and, like everyone else, he wanted to rule.

When James did not get to rule, he went away to sulk, and managed to be readmitted to his Spanish prison. He died in 1375. After James Joanna chose Otto of Brunswick, a soldier with no claims to rule who she thought would help defend her country. She was always threatened by revolts led by whichever Durazzo or Taranto happened to be adult and not yet executed at the moment; and from time to time outsiders like Louis of Hungary attacked her.

When Louis threatened her again Joanna decided to chose an heir who could help her. All her close kin having died or been executed, she selected Louis of Anjou, brother of King Charles V of France, but Louis of Anjou failed to help her in time when Louis of Hungary attacked in support of his choice of heir, Charles of Durazzo. Otto proved to be a washout as a soldier: Charles captured Joanna and imprisoned her. When Louis of Anjou led his army to rescue her, Charles announced that Joanna had died a natural death. This was true, since it is natural for someone held between two feather beds to die for lack of air. After her suffocation, Joanna's unmarked body was shown to her subjects to convince them that they had no alternative to supporting Charles.

ISABELLE OF BAVARIA
1371-1435

Isabelle of Bavaria made herself the most hated Queen that France ever had. The only person who has ever praised her was the Marquis de Sade, who liked her cruelty, and thought, mistakenly, that she was intelligent enough to have planned her crimes.

Isabelle entered France in 1385, when she was sent on approval to King Charles VI, who was seventeen; he had been king since he was twelve. As soon as he saw Isabelle, he wanted to marry her instantly. He could hardly sleep till the marriage was consummated. He may have inspired the proverb, "Marry in haste, repent at leisure."

The marriage was happy enough until August, 1392. King Charles led his army on a hot day across a sandy plain. He was wearing full armor, covered by a black cloak. A sudden alarm frightened him, and he went mad. He killed four of his courtiers before his companions were able to overpower him. He remained insane for five months: this was the first of forty-four episodes of madness, which occupied most of the rest of his life. While his body remained healthy, he was increasingly unable to understand political matters. He did whatever those who were with him told him to do.

French politics became a rivalry for custody of the King. Isabelle was in the middle of this. All she wanted from life was to have her desires gratified. She had no real interest in the Kingdom of France: indeed, she never bothered to learn to speak French well. She would cooperate with anyone who would assure her the right to dip into the Treasury whenever she chose.

She formed a close alliance with her husband's brother, Louis, Duke of Orleans, whose mistress she became. Together they governed the kingdom. But Louis was opposed by his cousin Jean *Sans Peur* ("the Fearless"), Duke of Burgundy. The arrogant Louis had seduced Burgundy's wife, and the two hated each other. Their relatives tried several times to reconcile them: the last occasion came in November 1407.

ISABELLE OF BAVARIA

A dress borrowed from Anne of Burgundy; Bedford Hours, British Museum.

After the effigy from the Great Hall of the Palais de Justice, Poitiers.

Orleans and Burgundy swore friendship. The next day Orleans went to visit Isabelle, whose baby son, the last of her twelve children (mostly by the mad king), had just died. After supper he left, responding to a message calling him to the King's mansion. Louis rode down the dark street singing, tossing his glove up in the air and catching it, by the light of the torches his companions bore. Fifteen men with swords and axes attacked his party in a dark street. "Stop! I'm the Duke of Orleans," Louis cried. "That's just what we wanted to know," one answered, as they scattered his brains across the cobblestones. Then the attackers fled into the night, strewing caltrops to block pursuit.

The princes of the royal family were called, and kept vigil with the body that night. Burgundy, who had hired the assassins, was among them: he "made above others every loud lament," weeping and sobbing. When his complicity was revealed, he ceased mourning and fled to his Duchy of Burgundy, from which he returned with an army to take control of Paris, the King, and the government. He brought with him a monk who preached a sermon explaining that Louis had been a tyrant, and it was every man's duty to kill tyrants, so Burgundy was not a murderer.

As Louis' widow did not agree, a feud began between the Burgundians and the party supporting Louis' widow and young son. They were led by the Constable of Armagnac, a talented but violent and brutal man, and were known as the Armagnacs. First one party, then the other, controlled France. The English, under King Henry V, invaded the kingdom and destroyed the French army at Agincourt in 1415.

At this point the Armagnacs held control of the Government. Isabelle, now forty-five, was pathologically fat, unable to get around without a wheel chair. She lived outside Paris at Vincennes, where she was free to do as she chose with her three lovers, the principal one of whom, de Bosredon, was half her age. As she wanted more money, she began plotting with the Duke of Burgundy. When Armagnac detected her plot, he told the King about her lovers. Charles usually accepted events passively; but spurred on by his only surviving son, the Dauphin Charles, the King grew angry. He, the Dauphin, and Armagnac rode to Vincennes, where they arrested Bosredon, who was tortured, strangled, and thrown into the Seine in a sack. The Dauphin called his mother names and asked her who had been his father; Isabelle called him the feebleminded son of a madman, which answered his question.

The Dauphin and Armagnac imprisoned Isabelle with few comforts and without the lovers she craved. She managed to send an appeal for help to the Duke of Burgundy—the same duke who had murdered her former lover, Orleans—and Burgundy sent troops to rescue her. Under Burgundy's protection and control Isabelle took the title of Regent of France, and set up her own court and parliament at Troyes. Her new lover, Jean de Villiers de l'Isle Adam, swore that he would revenge her on the Constable d'Armagnac, and when spies betrayed Paris to the Burgundians, who massacred the Armagnacs in the street and regained possession of the King, he did. Villiers killed Armagnac in prison, leaving the cross of Burgundy on his chest.

The Dauphin managed to escape Paris before the massacres and set up his own parliament at Poitiers. He and Burgundy negotiated distrustfully, while Henry V conquered Normandy. In September 1419 a meeting between the Dauphin and Burgundy at the Bridge of Montereau ended in the murder of Burgundy. In quest of vengeance his followers and the new Duke allied themselves with England. The result was Isabelle's last and most infamous sellout, the Treaty of Troyes, in May 1420. Henry V was given Isabelle's daughter Catherine in marriage, and was recognized as the adopted son of Charles VI and Isabelle, and as their heir. He would rule France as Charles's regent. The Queen would receive a pension—all she cared for. In return, she asserted that her son the Dauphin was illegitimate, and thus not entitled to the French crown. The treaty describes him as "Charles, who calls himself the Dauphin."

The Treaty of Troyes failed to control France's future, partly because both Henry V and Charles VI died in 1422. Isabelle no longer had any power. She survived another thirteen years, watching impotently as her hated son reclaimed his kingdom from the infant Henry VI and his regents. The conquerors took everything from Isabelle, who lived in poverty on a small English pension. She died repudiated by her son, abandoned by the Burgundians, despised by the English, and loathed by the French.

MARGARET OF ANJOU

We will not from the helm
to sit and weep,
But keep our course, though
the rough winds say no.
—Shakespeare

For more about medieval women, see our *Wife of Bath.*

From the Master of the Aix Annunciation, c. 1445.

Face, from a medal by Pietro da Milano, 1463.

MARGARET OF ANJOU
1430-1482

Like many infamous women, Margaret would never have won her fame without the aid of the man she married. King Henry VI, who was born in 1421, inherited the thrones of England and France before he was one year old, and spent the rest of his life losing them. While he was a child, the French began to take back their own country, which had been conquered by his father, the glorious Henry V. England had too few troops and too little money to defeat the French, but no one in England was ready to accept defeat as inevitable. Two political factions fought for power. The first, headed by Henry's uncle Humphrey, Duke of Gloucester, advocated defeating the French in battle, just the way England had always done. As they were never in power, they never had to figure out how to do this. The other group, headed by various more distant relatives of the King, wanted to make peace with France on terms whereby the French would let the English keep what they had left. This policy, like the first, failed for lack of French cooperation.

But the peace policy led to the introduction of Margaret into England. Her aunt was the Queen of France, and it was assumed that a marriage between Margaret and Henry might bring peace. The King of England seemed to be a matrimonial prize, but when Margaret got to England after her marriage in 1445, she found she'd won the booby prize. In addition to inheriting France from his grandfather, Charles VI, Henry had inherited his tendency towards feeble-mindedness. He caused no trouble: when sane he was kind-hearted, pious, and rather afraid of women. When a court lady in a low-cut dress came near, Henry said, "Fy, fy, for shame!", blushed, and fled. He liked to give things away, and disliked punishing criminals or fighting battles. More successful kings of the period took the opposite approach to these matters. When Henry was insane, he was even less trouble, as he sat about doing nothing.

Margaret was good-looking and energetic. She liked to hunt—animals and property in particular. She quickly took control of Henry, and made him favor the party that had promoted her marriage. Property belonging to the other party she regarded as fair game. Duke Humphrey was arrested in 1447. He died in prison two days later, reportedly of a stroke: people noticed that Margaret took possession of some of his estates the next day, and drew unkind conclusions.

Humphrey's position as leader of the opposition was inherited by Richard, Duke of York, a royal kinsman whom many believed to have a better claim to the throne than Henry. Margaret hated him and his family, and tried in every way to weaken their power. Her persecution eventually drove them to rebelling against Henry's rule to avoid being killed.

A truce came when in August 1453, Henry went mad. In October Margaret's only child, Edward, the Prince of Wales, was born. When the baby was shown to the King, Henry said that the Holy Ghost must have done it—which led Margaret's enemies to assert that the child was illegitimate. Margaret wanted to be regent during her husband's madness, but most people objected to having a woman—and a vindictive one at that—as their ruler. In March, 1454, Parliament made the Duke of York regent. He ruled rather well until, to the regret of everyone but Margaret, Henry recovered his sanity in January 1455.

With Henry's recovery, Margaret returned to power. Soon she managed to drive the Yorkists into rebellion, and what is called the War of the Roses began. Margaret led the Lancastrian side, dragging poor Henry about the countryside and into battles where he would refuse to fight, and pray instead. As a general, Margaret was brave but stupid. Her troops were so ill-disciplined that they usually did more damage to their friends than to their enemies. Margaret also lost popularity by pawning bits of English land such as Berwick (to the Scots) or Calais (to the French) in exchange for aid.

Her fortunes were up and down. At one point Margaret was captured by bandits: while they divided her property, she rode off and escaped with her son and a fourteen-year-old boy who was her guide: all three were on the same horse. While Margaret's army managed to kill the Duke of York in a battle, York's son took control of the country, and was crowned as Edward IV in 1461. Margaret retreated into Scotland. After being shipwrecked on a return from a trip asking for French help, she arrived back in Scotland in an open boat with her son, and continued to lead small attacks in the north of England, with Scottish aid—the kiss of death as far as English popularity went.

When Henry was captured, Margaret & Edward retreated to France, where they lived in exile 7 years, Margaret bringing up her son to hate her enemies. The tide turned again when Edward drove out of the country the Earl of Warwick, who had been one of his most powerful supporters. Margaret and Warwick hated each other as much as they could—and Margaret was a good hater. But Louis XI told them he would only offer help if they agreed to cooperate

Warwick led an army back to England; Edward fled, & the Lancastrians seemed triumphant. But Margaret was slow in returning to England with her son, and Edward IV returned first. Warwick was killed in battle the day Margaret and her son landed in England. Undaunted, she raised an Army. But Edward caught her at Tewkesbury in 1471. Her son was killed in the battle; Margaret was captured & hauled through the streets of London. Her husband was murdered in the Tower of London, and Margaret was a prisoner for five years. Edward treated her more kindly than she would have him. As he had no use for her, he finally sold her to Louis XI, who said he wanted to free his relative. After freeing her from England, he freed her from her possessions. In exchange for a pension, she signed over to him—not entirely willingly— her right to inherit any of her family's land in France. She lived the rest of her life in poverty and isolation in Anjou, and died in 1482.

LUCREZIA BORGIA

From a portrait in S. Giorgio Maggiore, Ferrara.

Lucrezia Borgia, the daughter of Pope Alexander VI, has a very bad reputation. The Contemporary Florentine historian Guicciardini says that she slept with her father and two of her brothers; others accuse her of numerous love affairs and of complicity in the Borgia poisonings. According to their enemies the Borgia family had the secret of a slow poison, *cantarella*, with which they decimated Rome. Alexander

Dumas claims they made it by feeding a bear arsenic, waiting till the bear threw up, and then suspending the bear head downward to collect the foam from its mouth—an unlikely process, and very difficult to perform secretly in the Vatican.

Actually, of course, the Borgias were involved in Italian politics in a period when everyone played very hard ball indeed. Few actions were ruled out as too dirty, and nothing was too vile to accuse your opponents of. So one can't believe everything said by the Borgias' opponents.

Most of what happened in Italian politics at this time resulted from the rivalry between France and Spain for control of Italy. The rulers of the various small Italian states allied in turn with France, Spain, and each other in attempts to keep their possessions. As the Pope ruled the central part of Italy, he too was involved in this diplomacy and warfare.

Lucrezia's father, Cardinal Rodrigo Borgia, was chosen Pope in 1492, and took the name Alexander VI. Borgia was sixty: a Spaniard, he had achieved rapid promotion in the church after his kinsman Alonso became Pope Calixtus III in 1455. At twenty-five Rodrigo was a Cardinal, and the Vice-Chancellor of the Church, the second highest office in the Vatican. An efficient administrator and a jovial companion, Rodrigo enjoyed the good things of life. In consequence he found himself with a number of children, something which a Cardinal is not supposed to have.

After Rodrigo became Pope, his children became prominent. As he was fond of them, he looked for good things to give them. Cesare, about eighteen, was put into the Church, where his father could provide for him: he became a Cardinal in 1493. Juan, who was about sixteen, was made Duke of Gandia, succeeding to a title held by a dead half-brother. Negotiations began for a marriage for Lucrezia, who was twelve, and for provisions for her brother Jofre, who was eleven.

Lucrezia was a pretty, delicate girl with blonde hair so long that its weight sometimes gave her a headache. Then as now the Italians admired blondes, who had scarcity value. She was also intelligent, with a taste for the new art and literature of the Renaissance. Just before her father became Pope, engagements had been made for her, first with one man, then another; these were broken, as her value had increased, and she was awarded to Giovanni Sforza, a kinsman of the rulers of Milan, who wanted an alliance with the Pope in case of a French invasion.

In 1493 Lucrezia, aged thirteen, married the twenty-eight-year-old Sforza in a splendid ceremony at the Vatican. She wore her long fair hair down to her waist. Soon after her brother Jofre was married to Sancha, the illegitimate daughter of the heir to the throne of Naples; the Neapolitans wanted an alliance with the Pope too.

Lucrezia's marriage was put on shaky ground when the Milanese made an alliance with the French and helped the French invade Italy. The Pope allied himself with Naples against them. Now Lucrezia's husband was in the uneasy position of having ties with both sides. He decided to play both sides: taking a job commanding troops for Naples, he sent as much information as he could to his kinsmen in Milan. He stayed away from his shrewd father-in-law whenever possible.

In 1496, after the French had temporarily been thrown out of Italy, the Borgia family gathered in Rome. The Pope had decided to attack the powerful noble families of the Papal states in order to reassert papal control and wanted people around him whom he could trust. His son the Duke of Gandia was to command his troops. Cesare was there too, involved in a torrid affair with Jofre's wife Sancha. The Pope also decided that if Lucrezia were free of her unsatisfactory marriage, he could use her hand to bind a new alliance. He decided the marriage would be annulled, on the grounds that it had never been consummated. It took some time to bully Giovanni into swearing this, as it was a lie, and he felt it impugned his masculinity, but he was a timid man, and gave in. He claimed that the Pope wanted Lucrezia all for himself.

During this period, Sancha ceased her affair with Cesare in favor of one with Gandia. On the night of June 14, after a Borgia family party, Gandia went off to a tryst. He was never seen alive again. His body, full of dagger wounds, was found in the Tiber. No one knows who killed him: some think that Cesare decided that his brother stood in his path, and removed him. The Pope, who was agonized at Gandia's

A Dress for Lucrezia Borgia

A dress borrowed from Lodovica Tornabuoni, from a painting by Ghirlandaio; Santa Maria Novella, Florence.

death, cut short the investigation, which suggests he feared learning the truth.

While temporarily unmarried, Lucrezia had an affair with a Spaniard, Pedro Caldes, who made her pregnant. When Cesare discovered this, which lowered her value in the marriage market, he chased Caldes through the Papal apartments with a dagger, finally trapping him in front of the Papal throne, where he stabbed him. "The blood spurted into the Pope's face." Later the bodies of Caldes and of Lucrezia's lady-in-waiting, who must have helped the affair, were found in the river.

After this entanglement had been ended, Lucrezia was married in 1498, age eighteen, to Alfonso of Aragon, Sancha's brother, another bastard of the Neapolitan royal line. The groom was made Duke of Bisceglie: the couple settled down together happily in Rome, until another shift of political alliances made his position dangerous. When the Pope seemed to be forming an alliance with the French against Naples, Alfonso left his six-months-pregnant wife and fled to Naples. He wanted Lucrezia to join him there, but her father gave her a job instead: he made her Governor of Spoleto and Foligno, north of Rome, and sent her there to govern.

In 1499 the French reinvaded Italy, now as allies of the Pope. They lent him troops, which Cesare commanded, and the Pope began to take over direct rule of various cities in the Papal states. Cesare became very powerful.

Lucrezia had her baby, who was baptized Rodrigo, after his grandfather, in the Sistine Chapel. Alfonso returned to Rome, where Cesare was eliminating people. His former favorite soldier was found in the Tiber one morning, with his hands tied behind his back and a sack over his head. He knew too much.

In the Jubilee Year of 1500, as pilgrims crowded into Rome (among them Martin Luther), Cesare decided to eliminate his brother-in-law. On July 15, Alfonso walked out at early evening: three assassins attacked him outside St. Peter's. He was wounded severely, but saved by the Papal Guards. Lucrezia, who fainted at the news, nursed him faithfully with the aid of Sancha. They prepared Alfonso's food themselves to avoid the risk of poison. Alfonso was recovering well when on August 18 Lucrezia and Sancha left him with friends. When they returned, Cesare's soldiers had taken possession of the sickroom. They were told that Alfonso had died of an "accidental fall" which had reopened his wounds. He was buried hastily that night. Now Lucrezia was available again for her family to offer as part of a treaty of alliance.

She was given finally to her best-born husband, Alfonso d'Este, heir to Duke Ercole of Ferrara. His family had ruled Ferrara for nearly four hundred years: they were proud, capable, and pious people. This marriage they regarded as beneath their dignity, but the Pope offered an enormous dowry from church funds, and they feared that if they rejected the alliance, Cesare's army would take Ferrara from them.

Lucrezia spent the rest of her life in Ferrara. Her husband kept her pregnant most of the time, and her health suffered. But she enjoyed the cultured court, which often housed such distinguished poets as Aretino, Ariosto, and Bembo, and her husband's power protected her from the ruin which overtook her family in August 1503. Cesare and the Pope went to a party given in a vineyard on a hot day. A number of the guests became very ill afterwards. The Pope died, and Cesare was so ill that he was unable to control the conclave held to elect the new pope. The rumors said that he and his father had been poisoned by wine which they had prepared to kill others, but medicine was so primitive at this time that all illnesses of prominent persons were attributed to poison.

The new pope was an enemy to Borgia power. He took away Cesare's conquests, and the rest of Cesare's life was an anticlimax. Betrayed to his enemies in Naples, imprisoned in Spain, he escaped and died fighting in a petty war on the Navarrese border. Lucrezia, who for some reason was fond of Cesare, was unable to aid him in his troubles, though she tried; she had little power of her own.

After one last love affair with her brother-in-law, ended when her go-between was found dead in the streets of Ferrara with twenty-two dagger stabs in him, Lucrezia became religious. She joined the Third Order of St. Francis, and wore a hairshirt under her clothes. She died in 1519, failing to recover from childbirth. As far as one can tell, she was only mildly infamous for her period. Her love affairs seem trivial offenses. She seems to have been a charming lady with some intelligence whose unscrupulous relatives used her ruthlessly to advance the interests of their family—more a victim than a villain.

ROXELANA

This majesty which appears in her face doth cover it may be a wicked and base soul.
M. De Scudery

From a minature by Reis Khaidara, Topkapi Gallery, Istanbul.

After a woodcut by Melchior Lorch, 1587.

ROXELANA
?-1558

By great talent in using her great beauty, Roxelana became the ruler of the most powerful and successful ruler of his age. Suleiman I of the Ottoman Empire, known as "Suleiman the Magnificent," came to the throne in 1520 at the age of 26 and ruled until 1566 with great success in peace and war. While Suleiman won his great victories, capturing Rhodes from the Knights of St. John in 1521, taking Hungary in 1526, and besieging Vienna with an army of 200,000 men in 1529, another war was waged in his harem. The Ottoman sultans had the tradition of never marrying: their children were the offspring of harem slaves. The queen of an early ruler of their line had been captured by enemies, and the humiliation had been so great that the dynasty resolved to prevent a repetition by having no more queens. So instead the ruler kept three hundred girls in his harem, most of whom had been captured in war or bought in the market. When they expected a visit from their master, they dressed in their finest robes and stood in line to receive him. He placed his handkerchief on the shoulder of the one who most pleased him, and retired with her. The next morning she would be presented a dress of cloth of gold, and her allowance would be increased. A harem girl who did not catch the sultan's eye by the age of twenty-five was freed and released to marry elsewhere.

Catching the sultan's eye was the road to fortune, but those who had his favor worked hard to keep it. In the early days of Suleiman's reign the favorite concubine was a Circassian girl known as "The Rose of Spring." By her Suleiman fathered Mustapha, his acknowledged heir, a handsome and talented youth. The Circassian defended her position: when a young Russian captive, Khurrem ("The Laughing One") with beauty, gaiety, and cleverness, whom we know as Roxelana, was favored by the sultan once, she ordered the girl never to let the sultan see her face again. Harem favorites often enforced such orders by the use of poison: their servants were ready to kill to defend the position of their mistresses. But Roxelana refused to obey. After her face was marked in a fight with the Circassian, she managed to be seen by Suleiman, who inquired into the cause of her disfigurement. Her triumph, and the disgrace of her rival, followed.

Now the acknowledged favorite, she wanted more. In 1533 Mehemet, her son by Suleiman, died. She and the emperor both felt great grief, and Suleiman gave Roxelana rich presents to console her. She used them to build a mosque; but when she asked if she was acquiring credit in heaven, the ministers told her that all good deeds done by a slave are credited in heaven to her master. Suleiman freed her, on hearing this; she then refused to sleep with him, since Islamic law said that only a wife or a slave could morally sleep with a man. The Emperor found himself forced to marry her and make her his empress, in 1544, even though the act was contrary to the policy of his dynasty.

Roxelana worked to improve her position. Suleiman's most faithful and talented servant was his principal minister, his brother-in-law the Grand Vizier Ibrahim, a Greek. He was not only the servant, but also the friend of his master and, with the aid of Suleiman's gifts, rivalled him in magnificence. Roxelana hinted that the servant might desire to become the master. She continued to repeat her warnings; Suleiman finally believed them. In 1536 Ibrahim Pasha was found strangled in his bed. His royal friend had arranged his death so that he would never know what was happening to him.

Roxelana's next objective, having chosen a protégé to replace Ibrahim as Vizier, was to make one of her sons heir to the throne. In addition to hating Mustapha, the son of her old rival, she needed to replace him to make her sons secure, since when a new sultan came to the throne, he usually killed his brothers, who were potential leaders of rebellions. She got Mustapha, who was beloved by the troops and the people, exiled to be governor of Diyarbekir, and began to suggest to Suleiman that Mustapha was popular because he was building a party to rebel against his father.

Once Suleiman suspected this, Mustapha's fate was sealed. Suleiman assembled an army, which he pretended was for Mustapha to command against the Persians. He summoned Mustapha, who came with Geangir, the youngest of Roxelana's sons, his close friend, who feared for Mustapha's safety. Only Mustapha was admitted into the royal presence; he was disarmed first, while his brother waited anxiously outside. When Mustapha was shown into Suleiman's presence, four slaves strangled him as his father

CATHERINE DE' MEDICI

watched. When the body was displayed publicly as a warning to traitors, Geangir killed himself, saying to his father as he stabbed himself, "Monster, neither thou nor my guilty mother deserves children like us."

After Mustapha's death, Roxelana, who was thorough, had his young son Ibrahim killed as well. She sent a eunuch to do the job; he separated the boy from his mother and left him dead.

Tush, all shall die
unless I have my will.
—Marlowe

A Helmet & A Dress for
CATHERINE the GREAT

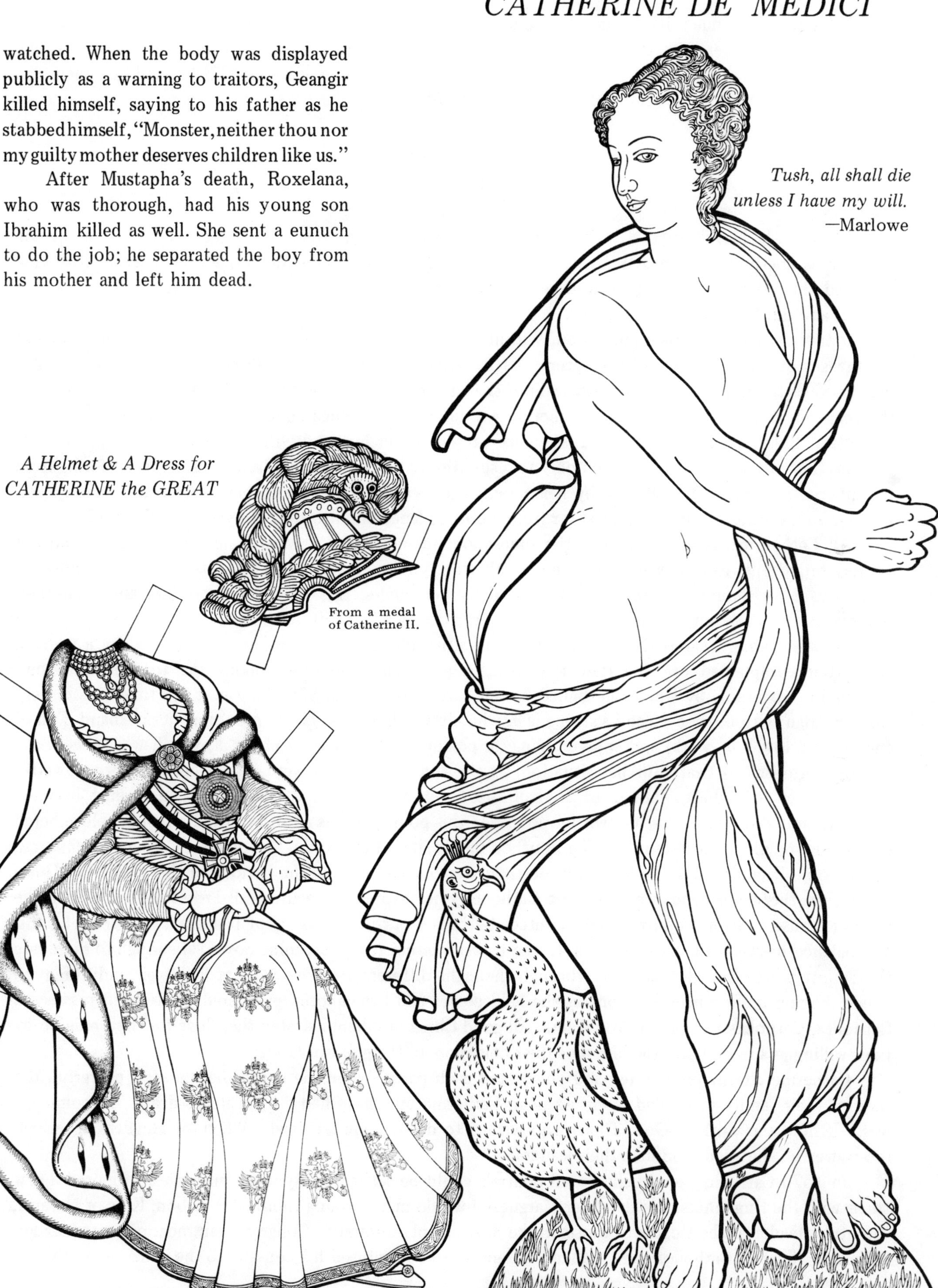

From a medal of Catherine II.

From the portrait of Catherine II by Torelli, c. 1762; Russian State Museum, Leningrad.

Catherine de' Medici as Juno, by the School of Germain Pilon; Musée de Cluny.

Roxelana continued intriguing. Her older son, Selim, was adopted as his father's heir. But she preferred her younger son, Bajazet, who was handsome, ambitious, clever, fawning, and deceitful. She sought ways to make him the heir, and no doubt only her own sudden death saved Selim and Suleiman. She died of a violent colic in the arms of her trusting husband.

CATHERINE DE' MEDICI
1519-1589

Niccolo Machiavelli argued in his *Prince* that a ruler should pursue his objectives without worrying whether his methods were moral: he dedicated the book to Lorenzo de' Medici, whose daughter Catherine followed this advice. She spent a lifetime using murder as a weapon in attempting to keep power, rule France, and put her children on thrones.

Catherine had a troubled childhood. Within a year of her birth in Florence, both her parents died of the ravages of syphilis. She survived several battles while growing up; in 1533 her uncle the Pope arranged her marriage to Henri, Duke of Orleans, son of the King of France, who became King Henri II in 1547. For the first ten years of their marriage, Catherine was unable to produce children. She was unimportant and powerless. But her position improved when she presented her husband with an heir in 1543—Francis. He was the first of ten children, of whom only two survived Catherine: her children were sickly, suffering from the inheritable diseases transmitted by her parents and Henri's. Gradually Catherine won status and power. But in 1559, during a tournament, a sliver from a broken lance ran into Henri's eye and killed him.

All Catherine's power was gone. Her oldest son was now King Francis II, at sixteen. Sickly and not terribly intelligent, Francis was dominated by his wife, young Mary Stuart (who later was better known as Mary Queen of Scots), and she was dominated by her uncles, the Guise family of Lorraine. But their dominance and Catherine's eclipse ended quickly: Francis died in 1560.

The new king, Charles IX, was only ten, and although the French disliked being ruled by a woman, and often complained of "the Italian woman," she became the ruler, taking the title of the king's *governante*—governor, by which she signed herself for the rest of her life. She was at this time a short, very stout woman with bulgy eyes and a strong jaw, who always dressed in black, mourning her husband. Full of energy, she loved to work, and enjoyed being in power. She was always cheerful, which was as well: she needed optimism to deal with her situation, as she and her children were caught between two powerful families, each of which wanted to control the government, using the religious controversy between Catholics and Protestants for its own purposes. At this point perhaps a third of the French people adhered to the new religion, Protestantism. The Bourbon family, next heirs to the throne after Catherine's children, had become Huguenots, as the French Protestants were called, and had the backing of this party. The Guise family, on the other hand, were extreme Catholics who favored persecuting all Protestants, and used the Catholic cause to gain the power they wanted. Catherine pursued a policy of peace between the religions, and balance between the rival families, trying to keep either from becoming powerful enough to dominate the country. She threaded her way through the eight different religious wars of her reign, indifferent to which religion predominated so long as she held power and her children prospered. Protestants massacred Catholics, Catholics massacred Protestants. All good Christians demonstrated their love for their religion by their willingness to dedicate the blood of their neighbors to the glory of God.

Catherine alternately favored and persecuted each party. When the Guises became too powerful, the head of their family was killed by an assassin. Catherine may have had a hand in his death: her comment was, "Behold the work of God. Those who wished to destroy me are dead." When the Huguenots became too powerful, she tried to kidnap their leaders.

In 1570 Catherine, who believed all quarrels could be settled by dynastic marriages, proposed a new truce with the Huguenots. Her daughter Marguerite would marry young Henri of Bourbon, King of Navarre, the titular leader of the Huguenot cause, in the presence of Admiral de Coligny, their most respected leader. Although all good Catholics were scandalized and the Pope refused his consent to the marriage, Catherine

A Dress for Catherine de' Medici

And if he grudge or cross his mother's will, I'll disinherit him and all the rest.

From a portrait of Catherine de' Medici in the Uffizi Gallery, Florence.

promised the Huguenots they would be safe, and they came to Paris for the royal wedding.

King Charles wanted to make himself independent of his mother's dominance. He found a father figure in Coligny, who wanted to end the religious wars in France by uniting the two sides against a foreign enemy. He filled Charles with the idea of winning glory by defeating the Spanish in Flanders. Catherine opposed the idea: she always favored peace, and doubted that the French could beat the Spanish. She and Coligny battled for control of the King. Coligny would gain the advantage in her absence, but when she returned her poor son could never stand up to her. A tubercular youth, he used up his frustrated energy in violent exercise and violent hunting. Charles liked the sight of blood, and when too ill to go hunting, would kill domestic animals about the court.

Catherine decided that she could retain her control of the King and the country by letting the Guises assassinate Cogligny, after which she expected that the Protestants, seeking revenge, would rid her of the Guises. Machiavelli would have approved the plot, but not its execution: the assassin whom Catherine loaned to the Guises only wounded the Admiral. The King ordered a royal investigation and swore revenge. The failure of Catherine's plot endangered her. She decided to save herself: on Saturday, August 23, at a meeting in the Tuilleries Gardens, she planned the murder of the Protestant leaders. After sending out orders to the Royal troops, and to the people of Paris, who hated the Huguenots, Catherine went to her son the King. She told him that he must either allow her plan to be carried out, or arrest her as one of the Admiral's assassins. Charles fought his mother, wanting to save his Protestant friends and preserve his Royal promise to protect the guests at the wedding, but his strength was not great enough to defeat his mother. He yelled, "Kill them all, so that not one will be left to reproach me afterwards! Let them all be killed!"

On the morning of Sunday, August 24, St. Bartholomew's Day, the churchbells rang at three a.m. as a signal. The massacre began with the murder of Coligny, who was stabbed in his room, thrown out a window, and kicked in the face as he was dying. His body was carried through the streets of Paris, with everyone stabbing at it. Then murder broke out in all the streets, and even in the Louvre, the Royal Palace, where many Protestant wedding guests had been offered hospitality and protection. Henri of Navarre, the royal bridegroom, was saved at Catherine's orders, as a future counterbalance to the Guise power, but was forced to renounce his religion. His friends were slaughtered in the corridors, or massacred in a courtyard, where the King looked down as they pled for his mercy. Charles IX is even said to have shot from his window at hunted Protestants running through the streets.

The Paris mob took up the pursuit of Protestants, private enemies, and loot, and the massacre continued in the streets until the 30th. In the provinces massacres continued some time longer. The final death toll was perhaps 3,000 in Paris, perhaps 10,000 in the rest of France: no one knows exactly. Catherine's comment on the whole bloody episode was, "Better that it should happen to them than to us."

But the massacre did not solve France's problems. Charles died at the age of twenty-four, in a bloody sweat, tortured by remorse. His last words were, "Ah, my mother."

He was succeeded by his brother Henri, the last Valois king. Henri liked to dress in women's clothing; when he was not associating with his perfumed favorites, known as the *mignons*, he walked in religious processions in which he whipped the back of the courtier in front of him, while the one behind the king tore his back with his whip. The Guises wanted Henri to call the Inquisition into France: Henri replied, "I prefer a heretic to a corpse. I won't have religion become a butchery, or the altar of God's sacrifice a shambles." The Guises pressed him: Catherine negotiated on his behalf with them.

At this point Catherine betrayed Henri, her only remaining son. He had confirmed as his heir Henri of Bourbon. She wanted her grandson, a Guise, the son of her daughter Claude, named heir. Encouraged by her astrologers, she believed that she would live many more years, and she planned to run the country again while her grandson grew up. Henri refused the treaty she had negotiated on his behalf, and had to flee Paris. Most of France was controlled either by the Huguenots, or by the Guisards. To preserve his throne, Henri had the Duke of Guise killed while he watched. The country rose against the King, and Catherine, seeing that all her life's work had resulted only in the death of a great many people, fell ill. She died thirteen days after the murder of Guise: no one had time to mourn. Her last son, Henri, was stabbed the same year.

FRANCES HOWARD

Countess of Somerset

I cannot be happy so long as this man liveth.

From an engraving by Renold Elstrack.

FRANCES HOWARD
1593-1632

In December 1613 Frances Howard married the handsome young Robert Carr, Earl of Somerset. She had wanted him for four years; she had used poison to achieve this marriage; now she expected to live happily ever after. The wedding was beautiful and expensive: the marriage of Carr, the favorite of King James I of England, with a daughter of the powerful Howard clan, one of the principal factions at court, had major political implications. Frances's family had long played the dangerous game of vying for royal favor. Several relatives who lost had been executed. Among her surviving relatives were the Earl of Nottingham, the Lord High Admiral, who had defeated the Spanish Armada, and had since profited by letting his ships rot; her great-uncle Henry, Earl of Northampton, the cunning old schemer who led the family; and her father Thomas, Earl of Suffolk, weak, stupid, greedy, and incompetent, who took his orders from that greedy shrew his wife.

Frances herself was beautiful, sweet, enchanting, and kittenish when she came to court in 1606. Her charm concealed the fact that she was uneducated, spoiled, and wilful—a dangerous combination. King James, who liked to make matches, married her off at thirteen to the fourteen-year-old Earl of Essex. Because of the couple's youth, they remained apart for three years. Essex went abroad, Frances stayed at court.

The year after her marriage twenty-one-year-old Robin Carr came from Scotland to the court. He was tall, handsome, athletic, and stupid. Carr caught the eye of the King, who liked handsome young men, during a pageant: Carr's horse misbehaved, and Carr was thrown with a broken leg. The King sent his own doctor to attend the handsome young man, then visited him and decided to train Carr to be a minister of state. He began instructing the invalid personally in Latin and statecraft. As Carr was no scholar, the Latin was abandoned, but the King thought there were still hopes for statesmanship. When Carr recovered he became the King's constant companion. "James leaned continually upon his arm, smoothed his hair, pinched his cheek, rearranged his clothes whenever they were disordered, and frequently embraced him in public." In exchange for whatever pleasures Carr gave the King, the King gave Carr everything that wasn't nailed down.

But how could one so stupid advise the King? Carr himself had a favorite, Thomas Overbury, who stagemanaged his rise. Overbury was a bright, ambitious, arrogant young man who wanted fame and power quickly. He had trained himself working for the government, but thought that by using Carr he could rise faster. He wrote Carr's letters, briefed him on the decisions that had to be made, and kept Carr from antagonizing powerful courtiers by telling him to be polite and humble. As Carr rose, Overbury went up with him, and people who wanted something from Carr came to Overbury.

Overbury decided that Carr must remain independent of the principal factions at court since his influence would be greatest if he aided first one side, then the other, in exchange for suitable rewards. If he sided always with one faction, he would become their captive. But Overbury's policy was ruined when Frances Howard fell in love with Carr. When her husband returned to set up married life, she refused to live with him. She turned to a childhood friend for help. Anne Turner, a pretty blonde widow, hung about the fringes of the court. She made dresses for court ladies, and set a style with her secret recipe for yellow starch stiffening in ruffs and sleeves. She also had good connections in London's underworld, and court ladies came to her if they wanted a fortune-teller, a love philtre, or a go-between. Mrs. Turner found Frances a magician who gave her a potion to quell her husband's desire and another to kindle Carr's. By 1612, having managed to keep Essex from consummating their marriage, Frances lived in her own house, and was Carr's mistress. But she wanted more: she wanted to marry Carr.

First she got Mrs. Turner to hunt for someone to kill her husband. When this idea failed, Frances decided to have her marriage annulled, which would leave her free to marry again.

Overbury disliked this idea. He did not want to see Carr become the captive of the Howard faction, and told him jealously that he must not marry "that filthy base woman." They quarrelled; Overbury threatened to prevent the annullment by exposing Frances's adultery. To prevent this, Carr and Frances's great-uncle Northampton trapped Overbury into offending the King, who was always jealous of his

A Dress for Frances Howard

From an engraving by Renold Elstrack.

influence on Carr. April 21, 1613, the King sent Overbury to the Tower of London as a prisoner.

Overbury did not know that Carr had betrayed him, and kept smuggling him letters with clever schemes to persuade King James to release him. Carr kept telling him to be patient: he meant the King to hold Overbury safely confined until the annulment was attained.

Frances had a simpler idea for keeping Overbury quiet—kill him. Uncle Northampton helped her by getting the honest Lieutenant of the Tower replaced by Sir Jervis Elwes, a weak man who wanted to get ahead. They made Elwes pay £2000 for his new position, then had him hire Mrs. Turner's servant Richard Weston as Overbury's guard. Frances and Mrs. Turner procured a slow poison, which they tested on a cat, with results that pleased them, if not the cat. They gave Weston the poison, but Elwes, who was not in the plot, found him poisoning Overbury's food, was horrified, stopped him, and threw out the poison. Elwes did not know what to do: he did not want to be involved in a murder, but was afraid to accuse his patron Northampton, for fear of what might happen to him. Trapped, he said nothing, but closely watched Weston.

When nothing happened to Overbury Frances got impatient for results. The king had appointed a commission, headed by the Archbishop of Canterbury, to judge her annulment. As they met, Frances began sending dainties from her kitchen to "poor Sir Thomas." One messenger, a musician, dipped a finger into the oozing pie he carried: in the next week he nearly died, and all his hair fell out. Elwes threw away any food that came from Frances, but now and again something got through. Overbury began to suffer from stomach pains.

The Divorce Commission finally deadlocked. The Archbishop, an honest man, said that Frances had a bad case, and had not proved it at all. The case became a public scandal. King James appointed two more bishops to the Commission—both pliable, ambitious men.

Meanwhile Overbury began to suspect that Carr had betrayed him. As the Commission was about to meet again, he threatened to tell everything he knew. He had to be quieted. Mrs. Turner paid £20 to William Reeve, the assistant to Overbury's doctor, to put sublimate of mercury into a clyster (an enema) given to Overbury. Apparently Elwes knew that a new plot to kill "the scab" (his name for Overbury in his daily letters reporting to Northampton) was planned: he had Overbury's best tapestries hung in the prisoner's room, since everything in the room of a prisoner who died became his jailor's property.

On September 14 Overbury was given the poisoned clyster: he died the next day, after great pain. He was hastily buried; Weston went back to work for Mrs. Turner; Elwes got Overbury's tapestries; Northampton spread the rumor that Overbury died of the pox; and Carr and the Howards ruled everything at court. The Divorce Commission voted 7-5 that the Essex marriage was a nullity, and the loyal seven were paid off. One man, Bilson, had his son knighted: the son soon became known as "Sir Nullity Bilson."

Now haste was made to celebrate the marriage of the newly virgin Frances Howard to the newly made Earl of Somerset. Expensive wedding presents for the young couple, elaborate entertainments, and poems by such writers as Ben Jonson and John Donne graced the occasion. Frances, dressed as a virgin bride, was married to her lover by the bishop who had earlier married her to Essex.

The fruits of her triumph rotted quickly, however. Uncle Northampton died of gangrene, and nobody intelligent remained to guide the Howards and Carr. Carr became arrogant, even to the King, and spent so little time with him that his enemies were able to interest James in a new favorite—young George Villiers.

Rumors began to spread about Overbury's death. Elwes was questioned and told everything he knew. King James ordered an investigation. Weston, arrested, broke down and implicated Mrs. Turner. She too was arrested; the Howards tried frantically to stifle the investigation. But Frances and Carr were implicated, arrested, and sent to the Tower: Frances had hysterics when she was given Overbury's rooms.

Weston, Elwes, the druggist who sold the poison, and Mrs. Turner were all tried, condemned, and executed. By the judge's orders Mrs. Turner was dressed for her hanging in the yellow-starched ruffs she had made fashionable: so were her executioners. That ended that style.

Frances and Carr were tried and found guilty, although Carr had probably not known of the poisoning. But they were not executed: the King saved them. They remained imprisoned until 1621: they grew to hate each other, and Frances took a lover. Released, they were sent to their only remaining country house, where they lived together without speaking. Frances went mad and died squalidly in great pain; her husband survived amid the ruins until 1645.

Left: a court dress borrowed from Madame de Montespan after the engraving by Trouvain. Right: the face of Madame de Brinvilliers is after the sketch made of her by Charles Lebrun while she was on her way to execution. The dress for strolling in the country is after the engraving by Jean Dieu de Saint-Jean. All second half of the 17th century.

THE MARQUISE DE BRINVILLIERS
1630-1676

Marie-Madeleine d'Aubray learned as a child how to get what she wanted—pleasure, pretty things, status, and the money with which to buy these. A pretty, precocious child, she had the charm and intelligence to manipulate people. In 1650 she persuaded her father to arrange for her the marriage she wanted with Antoine Gobelin, Marquis de Brinvilliers, a rich nobleman of the family which owned the famous Gobelin tapestry works.

The marriage was a step up in the world for Marie-Madeleine: now in high society, she learned to spend money fast for the pleasures she wanted. She gambled for high stakes, and took lovers: her husband, who had his own mistress, did not object.

In 1659 her husband introduced to her a young Gascon adventurer, his friend the Chevalier de Sainte Croix. They quickly became lovers—openly and scandalously so. In 1663 her father, who hated scandal, used his official connections to get a *lettre de cachet*, an order for the arrest and confinement of Sainte Croix. These were readily available to persons in positions of influence, and were often used to deal with family scandals. After his arrest Sainte Croix was imprisoned in the Bastille for six weeks. There he shared a cell with Exili, a well-known Italian poisoner. Exili was often used by statesmen of the period as part of their policy, but at the moment the government thought him too dangerous to be at large. In their enforced intimacy, Exili and Sainte Croix became friendly: apparently Exili told Sainte Croix many of his secrets, and suggested to him that a man could make a good living by arranging the removal of unwanted people.

Sainte Croix had already dabbled with alchemy, his period's ancestor of chemistry. When he was released, he set up a laboratory and began working seriously with poisons. Marie-Madeleine dropped the affair with her childrens' tutor which she had begun to amuse herself while Sainte Croix was absent, and followed her lover's new interest. They decided to prevent further paternal interference with their lives by poisoning Papa d'Aubray, a step which would also provide Marie-Madeleine with money to pay her debts.

But before undertaking a murder where their motive would be so apparent, the two decided to experiment with the effects of poison. Marie-Madeleine began visiting the Paris charity hospital, the *Hôtel-Dieu;* she began bringing delicacies from her own kitchen to some patients, her "special children," as she called them. Some died rapidly, some slowly: at length, she was satisfied that she understood her poisons.

In 1666 her father fell ill. Marie-Madeleine was summoned, and went to help nurse him. Despite her devoted care, he became worse and worse. After twenty-seven to thirty doses of poison he died, thanking his daughter for her care with his last breath. The sudden legacy reduced her debts, but half of her inheritance went to Sainte Croix; she also resented that three-quarters of the estate went to her sister and her two brothers, when she had done all the work.

By now she seems to have become intoxicated with the sense of power she felt. Just to test the effects of the poison, she gave some to her maid, and to her own daughter (she disliked her anyway). They survived, since she was also testing the power of her antidote.

Sainte Croix, alarmed by her recklessness, took away her poisons, but agreed to accept her as a client for his thriving poison business: he would arrange the deaths of her two brothers, who lived together, and Marie-Madeleine would inherit another nice chunk of money. Her part was to persuade her brothers to hire a servant, La Chaussée. They did not know that Sainte Croix had trained the man as a poisoner. Soon after he entered the d'Aubray household, the brothers fell ill: they vomitted, their insides burned. La Chaussée nursed them devotedly, night and day, but they got worse. Both died: they left La Chaussée legacies, to thank him for his care.

Marie-Madeleine's financial problems were solved, but only temporarily. Her extravagance outran all expenses. And she had other problems: La Chaussée blackmailed her into sleeping with him, and she quarrelled with Sainte Croix, who tried to poison her. Recognizing the symptoms, she took the antidote. His business had expanded to the point where discovery was inevitable before long.

Sainte Croix escaped discovery by dying in his laboratory in 1672, apparently poisoned by something he was making. When the police examined his laboratory, they found various poisons labelled as belonging to Madame de Brinvilliers. La Chaussée broke under torture, and told everything he knew.

But Marie-Madeleine had fled when he was arrested. She had taken refuge in a convent in the independent state of Liège. When Louis XIV's army occupied Liège, she was lured out of her convent, and arrested. Enraged at having been tricked, she tried to kill herself by biting a piece from her wineglass and swallowing it. When this failed, she tried to seduce the soldiers of her guard.

After her trial, she was condemned to be taken in a dung cart to the place of execution, where she would be beheaded, and her body would be burnt. The dung cart annoyed her: it offended her pride. The mob howled with rage as she was carted to the scaffold. She spent an hour kneeling there with her head on the block, while the executioner cut her long hair to prepare for his stroke. A priest comforted her while she waited. At sunset the executioner removed her head with one stroke of his long sword.

My heart hates to be a single hour without love. . .

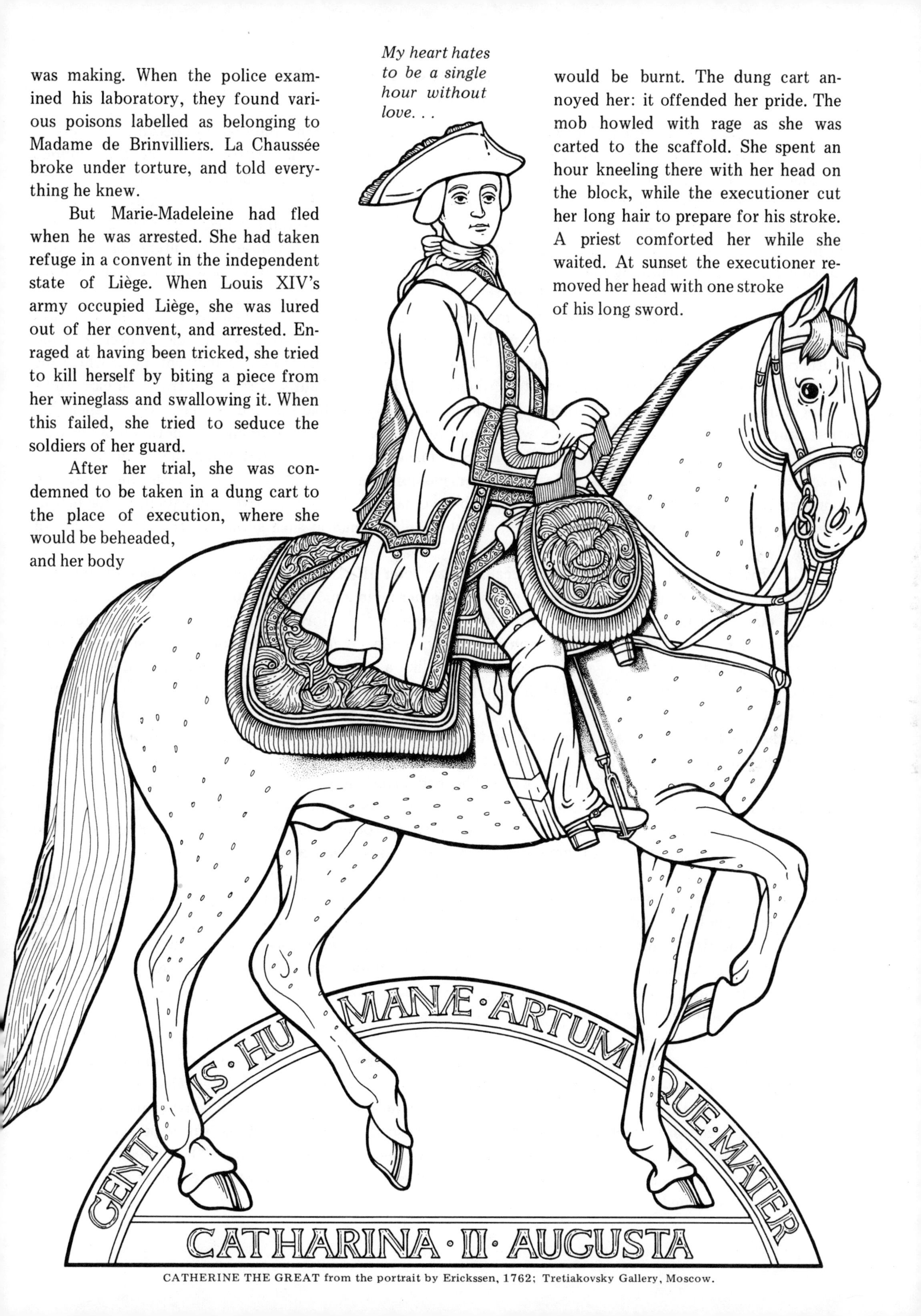

CATHERINE THE GREAT from the portrait by Ericksson, 1762; Tretiakovsky Gallery, Moscow.

EMPRESS CATHERINE THE GREAT
1729-1796

Sophia-Augusta of Anhalt-Zerbst, a daughter of a minor German noble family, became Empress of Russia with the aid of chance and an appetite for power. When she was fifteen the eccentric Empress Elizabeth (who had taken the throne in a palace coup) selected her to marry the heir to the Russian throne because Elizabeth had once been engaged to an uncle of Sophia's, and wanted to do his family a favor. But while marrying Peter, Elizabeth's nephew and heir, made Sophia the Grand Duchess Catherine and put her in line for the throne, it was a questionable favor. Peter was a stupid boor whose major interests in life were playing with soldiers, imitating the rigid military regulations of the Prussian army, and getting drunk. On his wedding night he passed out as soon as he hit the bed.

Peter also openly despised all Russians, and refused to learn their language. Catherine, who was ambitious, knew she needed supporters in Russia. She quickly learned Russian, and converted from Lutheranism to the Russian Eastern Orthodox Church. She endured the close confinement under which she and Peter were kept until she gave birth to an heir, Paul, in 1754. Paul was removed from her care, to be brought up by the Empress, and Catherine lived neglected, since she had fulfilled her purpose. She spent her time studying the various philosophers who wrote about the art of government and developing her own ideas on what needed to be done in Russia. She made some friends, and filled her time by taking lovers—three before her husband's death. In her memoirs she says, "I combined with the mind and temperament of a man the attractions of a loveable woman. . . . I was attractive; consequently, one-half of the road to temptation was already covered, and it is only human in such situations that one should not stop halfway."

In 1761 Elizabeth died, and Peter became Czar Peter III. He gave his mistress a place of honor at court, and began looking for an excuse to imprison Catherine in a monastery, after which he would divorce her and marry his mistress. Catherine, who was pregnant by her lover Gregory Orlov, a bright, reckless Russian soldier, remained patient and won sympathy, while Peter busily antagonized his subjects. Orlov persuaded the army to rebel against Peter, who fled like a coward; he was captured, abdicated, and was imprisoned. Shortly after, he was killed in prison, presumably with Catherine's approval. No one who knew him missed him.

Catherine took over the government, and began working fifteen hours a day at ruling Russia. Her major love was power: everything else was an incidental pleasure. She ate two meals a day, which were never luxurious, and spent her time at work. She had lovers—elsewhere in Europe they called her "the Messalina of the North"—but her lovers were used to help govern. She had an official lover, of whom there were between fifteen and twenty in her career. They lasted for an average of two years. Catherine trained them in administration, then sent them out as subordinates in various parts of the empire.

When she chose men, for whatever purpose, she had good judgment. Her lovers made good administrators. She selected the generals who gave Russia success in her wars, and who were to lead the Russians in defeating Napoleon. And she needed good men: she reorganized her country, recreated the army and the navy, began the first efforts at educating women in Russia, rewrote the laws, and put the church under the control of the government. She conducted an immense correspondance, taking advice from such philosophers as Voltaire and Diderot. In her spare time she wrote plays and fairy tales to amuse herself. She always had a gaity of spirit which made others enjoy her company.

After tidying up Russia, she decided to reorganize her neighbors as well. Poland was always turbulent: after she joined Austria and Prussia in partitioning it three times, there was no more Poland, and no more Polish problem. Russia got the lion's share of the country. When the Turks objected, Catherine beat them twice and annexed the Crimea to Russia. Her reign expanded Russia by 200,000 square miles and nearly doubled its population—which made her "Great" to those Russians who did not suffer personally in the process, and made her hated by her neighbors. She refused to accept the title "The Great" when her subjects offered it to her: "I do not choose to be called 'Great' in my lifetime. Such an epithet is for posterity to determine."

CHARLOTTE CORDAY

You will never use Madame on my letters; I shall never give up my beloved liberty; never shall any man be my master!

After the portrait by Tassaert, Bibliothèque nationale.

After the portrait by Hauer, Versailles.

CHARLOTTE CORDAY
1768-1793

Charlotte Corday earned her place in the catalogue of infamous women by assassinating Jean-Paul Marat as he sat in his bath on July 13, 1793. Charlotte was a well brought-up girl from Caen, descended from the poet Corneille, who felt that the French Revolution was going too far in 1793. For this she blamed Marat, a radical journalist and deputy of the National Convention. Marat believed fanatically in the dictatorship of the people. His newspaper, *The Friend of the People*, whipped up revolutionary fervour and helped provoke the September Massacres of 1792, in which mobs took over many of the Paris prisons and slaughtered more than 1,000 aristocrats, priests, common criminals and ordinary people who had the bad luck to be in the wrong place.

In 1793, the Girondists, a moderate faction, were turned out of the National Convention by the more radical Jacobins headed by Robespierre, Marat and Danton. Many fled to Caen, where Charlotte became obsessed with the idea that Marat was responsible for the Girondist downfall and the end of hopes for moderation.

Leading her father to believe that she was going to England, Charlotte set off for Paris. She bought a kitchen knife and called on Marat. She was allowed to see him after pleading that she needed his help and protection. He was soaking in the bathtub where he spent most of his time, trying to relieve the pain of a chronic skin disease. He said, "Misfortune, citizeness, has claims which I have never disregarded. Sit down." Instead, she stabbed him to death.

She was arrested immediately, tried on July 16 and executed the next day. She was 24. From prison she wrote to her father:

> Forgive me, dear Papa, for having disposed of my life without your permission. I have avenged many innocent victims; I have prevented numerous other disasters; the people will someday see this clearly and rejoice at having been delivered from a tyrant.

She also quoted from her ancestor Corneille: "It is crime that is shameful, and not the scaffold."

Marat had already retired from the National Convention because of his poor health, and his influence had been waning because he had become too fanatic even for such dedicated revolutionaries as Robespierre. Ironically, Charlotte Corday sacrificed herself to kill a dying man and by doing so, made him a martyred hero of the Revolution.

GEORGE SAND
1804-1876

George Sand's life now seems less shocking than it did a hundred years ago , but she managed to scandalize most people in her own time. She left her husband and lived openly with a lover, then left her lover, and lived more openly with other lovers. Instead of being ashamed of herself, she argued that she had as much right to live as she chose as men did. She dressed in men's clothes, smoked cigarettes and cigars like a man, and lived like a man on her own earnings. And worst of all, she was successful.

The girl who was christened Aurore Dupin was raised by her grandmother, from whom she inherited the family estate of Nohant in the province of Berry in France when she was seventeen. Next year she fell in love and chose a husband, Casimir Dudevant: marriage gave him control of her estate, and of her. She had been too young to choose intelligently: while Casimir was amiable, honorable, and a good father to their two children, his only interests were in shooting, drinking, local politics, and self-gratification. He bored her, and she found no fulfillment for the romantic expectations of life she had formed as a child.

She disliked the status of a married woman, and thought that women deserved equality in law and love. "Women are forced to lead a life of imbecility, and are blamed for doing so. If they are ignorant, they are despised, if learned, mocked. In love they are reduced to the status of whores. As wives they are treated more as servants than companions. Men do not love them: they make use of them, they exploit them, and expect, in that way, to make them subject to the law of fidelity."

From a drawing of George Sand by Alcide Lorenz.

A portrait of George Sand from the *Miroir Drolatique*.

Her first attempt to break out of the trap of marriage came when a handsome young man, Aurélien de Sèze, fell in love with her. They conducted an idealistic romance by letters, with no physical element, and with Casimir a party to all their meetings: they said he was the friend of both. All her life Sand was stimulated by situations in which two men were simultaneously in love with her.

This rather wispy affair satisfied no one. Casimir turned to drink, Aurélien to another woman, and Aurore to a local young man, Stephane de Grandsagne, whom she nursed through an illness. Love for Sand was always partly maternal, and a number of her lovers began as her patients. When she was twenty-six Jules Sandeau, a local boy of nineteen, fell in love with her. A weak youth, he needed a protector. The two went off to Paris together, and began writing to make a living. Since publishing under her own name would have been scandalous, because it would have led to publicity for her way of life, they used the pseudonym "Jules Sand." Their novel was successful, suiting the taste of the public which was just becoming enthusiastic about the new French Romantic writers. As Sandeau was rather lazy, his mistress had written most of the novel, and when she went to visit her children at Nohant, she wrote another, *Indiana.* This she published under the name of "George Sand" to capitalize on the success of "Jules Sand," while making clear that it was her own. From now on most people knew her by this name.

Indiana was a great success, praised by the best writers and critics of the day, even while the relationship with Sandeau was failing. He was idle, unfaithful, and jealous of her success. She broke with him, packed up his possessions, and sent him off on a trip to Italy. Her next great passion was with the handsome younger poet Alfred de Musset, a beautiful young débauché who, like many Romantic writers, found it necessary to destroy himself to get the material for his art.

Sand's love affairs were always run very domestically. Whatever else she did, she managed to find time to write eight hours a day, and usually wrote two or three books a year. Her lovers were organized so that they fit into her schedule, and she tried to make them as orderly and productive as herself. De Musset wrote one evening, "I had worked all day, and by the evening had produced ten lines and drunk a bottle of brandy. She, on the other hand, had polished off a litre of milk and written half a volume." Such tireless efficiency must have been irritating.

Sand and de Musset went off to Italy together, Sand having asked the permission of Alfred's mother to take him. She pushed him, and he achieved some of his best work under her influence. But they quarrelled. After they had decided to separate, he became ill in Venice, and she nursed him. While doing so, she fell in love with his doctor, Pagello.

When she returned to France, she took Pagello along. She had several reconciliations and partings with de Musset. Each in turn got tired of the other; the other, piqued by indifference, campaigned to recover the first. Finally, having exhausted all emotions of love and hate, they parted for good. After an involvement with a radical politician who favored killing the rich, but left Sand because he was afraid of his wife, and after some other unimportant men, Sand lived with Chopin, the great Polish pianist and composer. Ill, he wanted a mother and a nurse as much as a lover. She filled all these roles for him from 1838 to 1846. With her Chopin was as happy as his temperament ever allowed him to be. But they quarrelled and parted.

Sand continued active to the end of her life. She always wrote; she always attracted adoring younger men; she always enjoyed life, and took active part in it. When her first two grandchildren died of illnesses, she said to her son, "I *command* another child, for we must love, we must suffer, we must weep, hope, and create." While she became disillusioned with politics, and doubted the capacity of the French to govern themselves, she remained a republican. After outgrowing the ideas of her youth, she commented on the Romantic fever which had inspired her novels and her love affairs: "We despised paddling the shallows. What we wanted was to swim far out above unsounded depths, and the further we went, the more hopelessly lost we became. To get away from the ruck of our fellows, to put an ever greater distance between ourselves and the safe dry land, to push onward and onward—that is what we wanted."

Margaretha Zelle MacLeod, or

MATA HARI

Agent H-21

I have never done any espionage before. I have always lived for love and for pleasure.

Mata Hari's dress on the cover of *Nouvelle Mode*, 1913.

From a photograph, 1905.

MATA HARI
1876-1917

Mata Hari is famous as the beautiful dancer who seduced hundreds of men as a German spy so cunning that she found out every secret. In fact, however, she seems to have been just a woman with a talent for spinning self-promoting myths about herself, and her spying may have been just another fiction.

When Mata Hari became famous as a dancer in 1905, she told reporters different stories about her background. She claimed to have been born in the East—sometimes in India, sometimes in Java—where she had learned the sacred temple dances which she performed to glorify Siva. As these sacred dances required her to remove her clothes slowly, she impressed a number of critics, who enjoyed a culturally improving strip-tease. But all these stories were fiction. Mata Hari was born in a small town in Holland, as Margaretha Geertruida Zelle. Her father, a hatter and social climber, encouraged her to stand out by doing different and dramatic things. He went bankrupt in 1889; Margaretha's mother died in 1891; and Margaretha seemed headed towards becoming a kindergarden teacher when she met Rudolph MacLeod, a thirty-eight-year-old officer of the Dutch Colonial Army. Margaretha, half his age, liked his uniform.

Six days after they met, she was engaged to MacLeod. When they were married they went to the Dutch East Indies, where their marriage fell apart in a series of violent quarrels. In 1902 they returned to Holland and separated. Margaretha left their daughter with her husband and went off to Paris to achieve her childhood dreams of fame. After posing as a model, she decided to become an Oriental Dancer. She called herself "Lady MacLeod" and got a chance to perform at the Paris Museum of Oriental Art in March 1905. For this occasion she chose the name "Mata Hari"—Malay for the sun, "the eye of the day." She won fame by dancing completely nude and she became the vogue. She went on tour in Spain, appeared in a Massenet oriental ballet at Monte Carlo, danced in Vienna, danced at La Scala in Milan, and appeared at the Folies Bergère. A brand of cigarettes and a brand of biscuits were named after her and packed in tins with her picture on them. In every city lovers were eager to support her in the style which her invented background required. Some of them were famous men: in France, for example, her lovers included the Minister of War and the Secretary-General of the Foreign Office.

When World War I began in 1914, Mata Hari found fewer opportunities to perform, but more men in uniform. She decided to make money and become a heroine by spying for the Allies. The gossip she collected for the French was so trivial that they suspected her of being a German agent. The French arrested Mata Hari February 13, 1917: she was kept for eight months in a dirty, unheated, rat-infested cell while an obsessive spy-hunter questioned her and built up a dossier six inches thick. She was not allowed to see a lawyer or even to let her friends know she had been arrested.

The suspicious French considered everything evidence against her. Her prosecutor summed up the case by saying that her "facility of languages, innumerable connections, remarkable intelligence, and innate or acquired immorality all contribute to make her suspect. Without scruples, accustomed to make use of men, she is the type of woman who is born to be a spy." In other words, that she was an actress, and thus knew people all over Europe; that she spoke several languages; that she had not incriminated herself ("remarkable intelligence"); and that she was used to take care of herself by exploiting men rather than by being exploited by them, all proved that she must be a spy.

Seven military men were convinced, and condemned her to be shot. The thrifty French government also condemned Mata Hari to pay the cost of her investigation and trial: they sold her possessions and kept the proceeds. On October 15 Mata Hari was awakened at five a.m. and taken to Vincennes. She declined to be blind-folded or tied to the post as she faced the firing squad. She was shot at dawn. By executing her, the French convinced everyone that she had been a spy, and her name became a synonym for infamous vices. In fact she seems to have been just a rather silly woman with a gift for inventing romantic stories about herself which led to her career and her death.